THE CONQUEST OF THE WEST

A SOURCEBOOK ON THE AMERICAN WEST

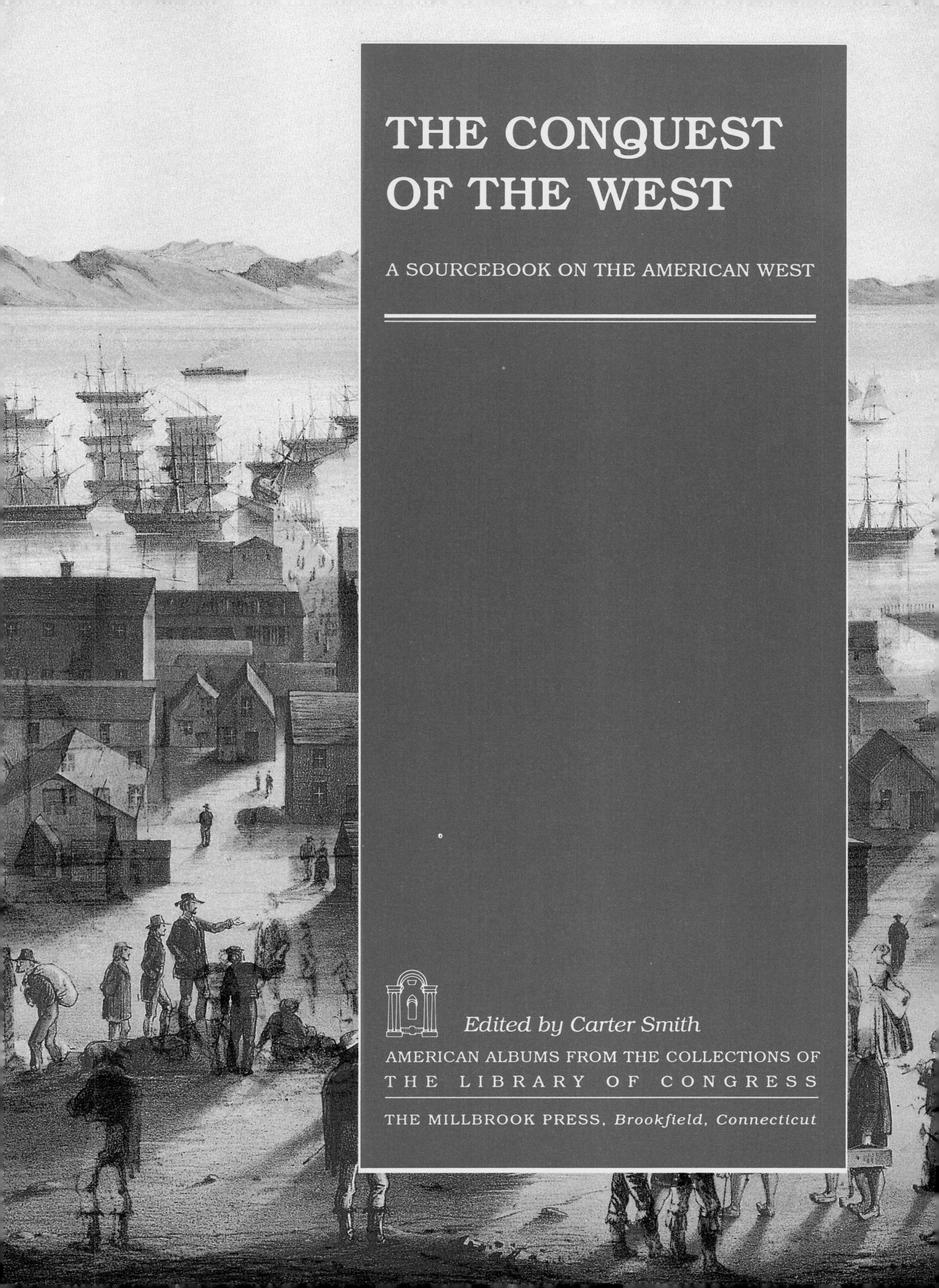

THE CONQUEST OF THE WEST

A SOURCEBOOK ON THE AMERICAN WEST

Edited by Carter Smith

AMERICAN ALBUMS FROM THE COLLECTIONS OF
THE LIBRARY OF CONGRESS

THE MILLBROOK PRESS, *Brookfield, Connecticut*

Cover: "The Storming of Chapultepec, September 13th." Color lithograph by Sarony & Major.

Title Page: "San Fransisco." Chromolithograph by M. & N. Hanhart, from a drawing by Samuel Francis Marryat, London, 1849.

Contents Page: Medal from the Indian Wars, 1907.

Back Cover: "Cutting Out Pony Herds," or "The Stampede." Painted in 1913 by Frederic Remington for the cover of Collier's Weekly *magazine.*

Library of Congress Cataloging-in-Publication Data

The Conquest of the West: a sourcebook on the American West / edited by Carter Smith.
p. cm. -- (American albums from the collections of the Library of Congress)
Includes bibliographical references and index.
Summary: Describes and illustrates the western territorial expansion of the United States, from post-Revolution territorial activities of the former thirteen colonies to the last military clashes in the early 1900s, through a variety of images created during that period.
ISBN 1-56294-129-1 [lib. bdg.]
1. United States--Territorial expansion--Sources--Juvenile literature--Sources. 2. West (U.S.)--History--Sources--Juvenile literature--Sources. [1. United States--Territorial expansion--Sources. 2. West (U.S.)--History--Sources.] I. Smith, C. Carter. II. Series.
E179.5.W543 1991
978--dc20 91-31130
CIP
AC

Created in association with Media Projects Incorporated

C. Carter Smith, *Executive Editor*
Lelia Wardwell, *Managing Editor*
Elizabeth Prince, *Manuscript Editor*
Charles A. Wills, *Principal Writer*
Kimberly Horstman, *Researcher*
Lydia Link, *Designer*
Athena Angelos, *Photo Researcher*

The consultation of Bernard F. Reilly, Jr., Head Curator of the Prints and Photographs Division of the Library of Congress, is gratefully acknowledged.

Manufactured in the United States of America.

10 9 8 7 6 5 4 3 2 1

Contents

When Thomas Jefferson, shown here, took office as president in 1801, the United States' western border was the Mississippi River. When he left office in 1809, the United States had doubled in size—thanks to the Louisiana Purchase, which Jefferson had authorized.

Introduction

THE CONQUEST OF THE WEST is one of the initial volumes in a series published by The Millbrook Press titled AMERICAN ALBUMS FROM THE COLLECTIONS OF THE LIBRARY OF CONGRESS and one of six books in the series subtitled SOURCEBOOKS ON THE AMERICAN WEST. They treat the history of the West from pioneer days to the early twentieth century.

The editors' goal for the series is to make available to the student many of the original visual documents of the American past which are preserved in the Library of Congress. Featured prominently in THE CONQUEST OF THE WEST are the rich holdings of early maps, prints, and original book and magazine illustrations preserved in two Library departments: the Geography and Map Division and the Division of Prints and Photographs. These pictorial records today offer a wealth of insight into their times, both in what they show and in how they themselves came about.

The opening of the American West coincided with, and was in fact made possible by, a communications explosion in the United States. The number of newspapers published in the United States multiplied enormously in the opening years of the nineteenth century, providing a vast network carrying news from the frontier to the most civilized parts of the East and back again. In the 1840s, illustrated magazines and weeklies became common, giving an added dimension to news reporting. Another medium which came of age during this period, lithography, also contributed to this explosion. This medium, which involved the printing of an image from a drawing made on a flat, polished stone surface, allowed the maps, political cartoons, portraits, and city views of the time to be produced far more quickly and cheaply than ever before. Lithography proved a versatile and valuable tool. Government expeditions surveying the West used it to reproduce for wide publication their detailed maps and drawings.

These images, becoming commonplace in American life, had a great impact on the way Easterners thought of the West, just as today they help shape our historical perspective. While some were scientific and factual, others were clearly biased. The political cartoons were produced not by independent observers, but by artists for hire who were paid by or who sought favor with the political parties of the day. The battle scenes of the Mexican War were produced by Currier & Ives and other firms in New York and Philadelphia—far from the battle front. Their purpose was less to present real events than to glorify the American cause and further the presidential aspirations of several future candidates, then commanding generals in the field.

After the Civil War, the portrayal of the West became heavily romanticized in the illustrated reporting of such artists as Frederic Remington, Clinedinst, and others. It was in their drawings for magazines such as *Harper's Weekly* that the exploits of the cowboy, the gunslinger, and the U.S. Cavalry were first celebrated.

The works reproduced here represent a small but telling portion of the rich record of Western life and achievements preserved by the Library of Congress in its role as the nation's library.

BERNARD F. REILLY, JR.

Part I: 1783-1836
Moving the Frontier West

The most famous of the early pioneers, Daniel Boone (1734–1820), is shown here rescuing his daughter from Indians in 1776. People of Boone's time viewed Western lands as theirs for the taking, although Indians had lived there for centuries.

"America," wrote historian John Knox Jessup, "was born with a noise at its back, the morning noises of three million square miles of virgin wilderness." This vast wilderness was the West.

Where did the West begin? For the earliest settlers in Virginia and New England, the frontier began just beyond their settlements on the edge of Massachusetts Bay or the Chesapeake Bay tidewater. During the colonial era, it was the Appalachian Mountains that marked the limit of settlement, until pioneers pushed across the mountains. By the end of the Revolutionary War in 1783, the western boundary of the United States was the Mississippi River. The stretch of land between the Appalachians and the Mississippi was inhabited only by Native Americans and a few traders and trappers, and many Americans believed it would take generations to settle this region. But within a few years permanent settlements filled the area, especially after the War of 1812 ended Britain's presence in the northern part of the region.

By that time, the frontier had shifted far west of the Mississippi. This was a result of the Louisiana Purchase of 1803, which doubled the size of the nation and pushed its western border to the Rocky Mountains. And, as if this vast new territory were not enough, Americans began moving into the Oregon Country and the Mexican province of Texas. In less than a lifetime, the United States had stretched itself across three quarters of the North American continent.

As part of the United States' first national census in 1790, the new federal government drew an imaginary boundary line down a map of the nation. To the east of this line were counties with populations of more than two persons per square mile; to the west, those with less. Of the nation's four million people, the census takers found, only six percent lived west of this "frontier line."

But that situation changed quickly. In 1860, the frontier line had shifted a thousand miles to the west in places. Now it ran through new states like Iowa and Kansas, Wisconsin and Texas—regions that were known only to their Native American (Indian) inhabitants and a few roving traders in 1790. And in 1860, half of the nation's population of 31,500,000 lived west of the frontier line laid down in the 1790 census.

In 1783, the United States' western boundary was the Mississippi River; by the middle of the nineteenth century it was the Pacific Ocean. The story of how this land was acquired is told in the different colors of the map reproduced here. But colors and lines on a map don't tell the whole story. The real story is one of back-room dealings in European palaces, as with the diplomatic efforts that secured the Louisiana Purchase. It is also one of violence—the Mexican War, the War of 1812, the countless battles with the Native Americans. For triumph and tragedy, few episodes in human history match the winning of the American West.

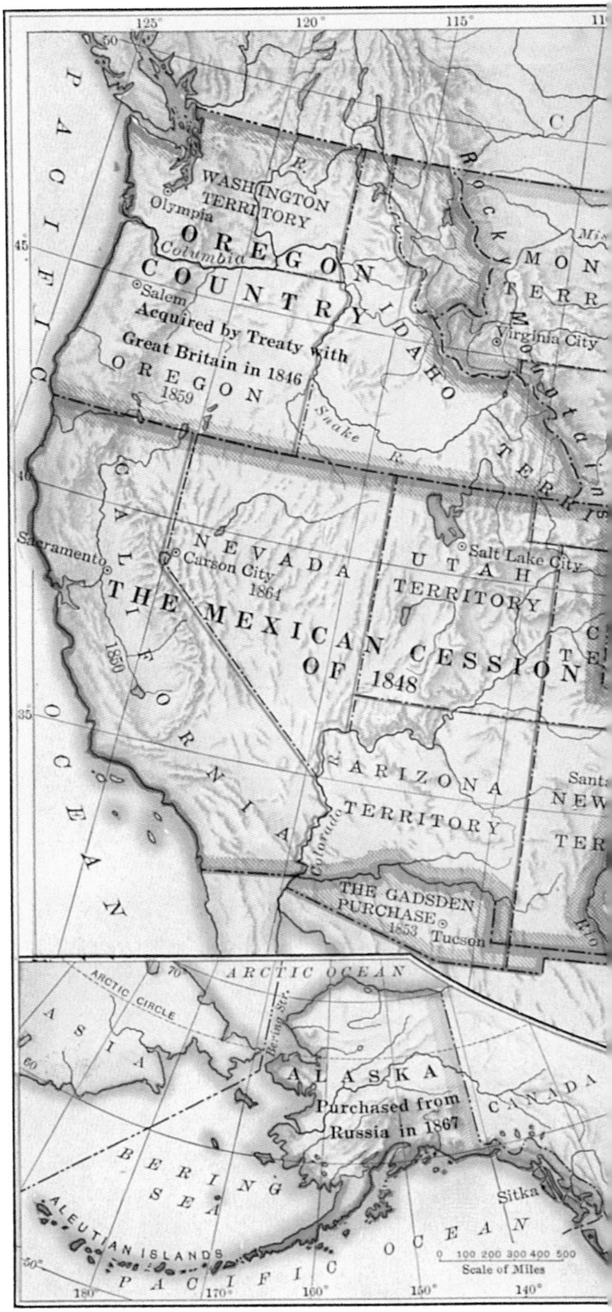

THE GROWTH
of the
UNITED STATES
From 1776 to 1867
The acquisitions made by the United States from 1776 to 1867 are shown by different colors.
The boundaries of the States and Territories at the close of 1867 are outlined by solid green lines:
The Capitals of the States and Territories in 1867 are shown on map by: ⊙
Scale of Miles
0 100 200 400 600
THE M.-N. WORKS.
100° Longitude West 95° from Greenwich 90° 85° 80°
105° 100° 95° 90° 85° 80° 75° 70°
CANADA
Lake of the Woods
Red R. of the North
River St. Lawrence
LOUISIANA Purchased from France in 1803
DAKOTA TERRITORY
NEBRASKA 1867
Lincoln
Yankton
KANSAS 1861
Topeka
INDIAN TERRITORY
TEXAS Annexed in 1845
Austin
MINNESOTA 1858
St. Paul
IOWA 1846
Des Moines
MISSOURI 1821
Jefferson City
ARKANSAS
Little Rock 1866
LOUISIANA 1812
Baton Rouge
WISCONSIN 1848
MICHIGAN 1837
Lansing
ILLINOIS 1818
Springfield
INDIANA 1816
Indianapolis
OHIO 1802
Columbus
KENTUCKY 1792
Frankfort
TENNESSEE 1796
Nashville
MISSISSIPPI 1817
Jackson
ALABAMA 1819
Montgomery
GEORGIA
Milledgeville
ACQUIRED BY CONQUEST DURING THE REVOLUTION AND BY TREATY OF 1783
THE THIRTEEN ORIGINAL STATES
FLORIDA 1845
Tallahassee
Acquired from Spain by Treaty in 1819
WEST VIRGINIA 1863
VIRGINIA
Richmond
NORTH CAROLINA
Raleigh
SOUTH CAROLINA
Columbia
PENNSYLVANIA
Harrisburg
Wheeling
MD.
Annapolis
Washington
DEL.
Dover
N. JER.
Trenton
NEW YORK
Albany
VT. 1791
Montpelier
NEW HAMP.
Concord
MAINE 1820
Augusta
MASS.
Boston
CONN.
Hartford
New Haven
R.I.
Providence
Newport
Golden City
COLORADO TERRITORY
MEXICO
GULF OF MEXICO
ATLANTIC OCEAN
Mississippi R.
Missouri R.
Ohio R.
Arkansas R.
Red R.
Platte R.
50 45 40 35 30 25

A TIMELINE OF MAJOR EVENTS

PART I *1783–1815 Moving the Frontier West*

UNITED STATES HISTORY

1783 The Revolutionary War ends when the U.S. and Britain sign the Treaty of Paris.

1784 James Madison argues for the separation of church and state in his pamphlet *Remonstrances Against Religious Assessments*.

1787 Delegates from twelve of the thirteen states draft the U.S. Constitution.

1789 George Washington becomes the first president of the United States.

1790 The temporary federal capital is moved from New York City to Philadelphia.

1791 The Bill of Rights is added to the Constitution.

1793 Washington and Adams are reelected president and vice president, respectively.

1796 Federalist John Adams is elected president and Democratic-Republican Thomas Jefferson is elected vice president.

1800 Washington, D.C., becomes the federal capital.

The Cumberland Road

1803 Congress grants funds for Meriwether Lewis and William Clark to lead an exploration expedition to the upper reaches of the Missouri River and westward to the Pacific Ocean.

1811 Construction begins on the Cumberland Road, the first major roadway funded by the federal government.

1812 Congress declares war against Britain when the U.S. is provoked by

THE CONQUEST OF THE WEST

1784 Congress adopts Thomas Jefferson's plan to admit Western regions to the Union as organized territories.
•Settlers led by John Sevier organize the State of Franklin, which later becomes Tennessee.

1787 Congress passes the Northwest Ordinance. It calls for the Northwest Territory (the land between the Mississippi and Ohio rivers) to eventually become three to five states and also prohibits slavery in the region.

1792 Kentucky becomes the fifteenth state.
•Captain Robert Gray, aboard the ship *Columbia*, lands on the coast of what is now Washington State. The U.S. uses this voyage as the basis for its claim to the Pacific Northwest.

Thomas Jefferson

1795 The U.S. and Spain sign the Treaty of San Lorenzo. It allows Americans to trade on the lower Mississippi River.

1796 Congress passes the Land Act, which sets a minimum price for the sale of government land to settlers.
•Tennessee becomes the sixteenth state. It is the first Western state created out of federal land, not land that was part of another state.

1798 The Mississippi Territory is organized.

1803 Ohio becomes the seventeenth state.
•After months of negotiations, the Louisiana Purchase is completed. For about $15 million, France sells more than 800,000

Britain's maritime policy in its war with France and by Britain's relations with Indians of the American Northwest.
•General William Hull and 2,000 U.S. troops are captured in Detroit by the British.
•The U. S. warship *Constitution* ("Old Ironsides") wins a major victory for the United States Navy by destroying the British frigate *Guerrière* on the St. Lawrence waterway.

1813 The Americans achieve an important victory as they capture York (now Toronto); the British destroy the fort rather than let it fall into the hands of the Americans.
•The British defeat an American force near Detroit, but

Andrew Jackson

the U.S. fleet under Captain Oliver Perry wins the Battle of Lake Erie, and the British must pull out of Detroit.
•British forces cross the Niagara River and burn Buffalo, New York, and surrounding areas.

1814 American general Andrew Jackson wins a victory at Horseshoe Bend, Alabama, and forces the Creek Indians to give up 22 million acres of land.
•Following their defeat of Napoleon, Britain sends over another 15,000 troops to defend Canada.
•Washington, D.C., is burned by the British; President Madison is forced to flee.
•The Treaty of Ghent is signed, ending the War of 1812.

1815 The U.S. government agrees to limit the number of peacetime military troops to 10,000.

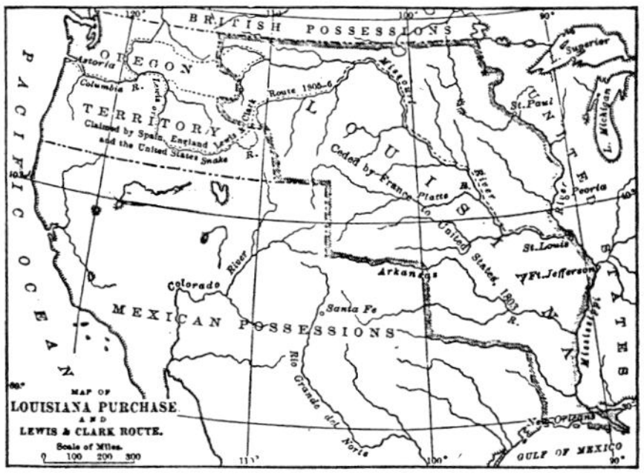

Map of the Louisiana Purchase

square miles to the U.S. The purchase doubles the size of the United States.

1811 The ship *Tonquin*, sent to the Pacific Northwest by millionaire John Jacob Astor, is destroyed by an explosion. This blocks Astor's plans for a fur trading empire in the region.

1812 British officials in Canada forge an alliance with the Shawnee Indian leader Tecumseh against American settlers in the West.
•The Territory of Orleans becomes the state of Louisiana; the rest of the Louisiana Purchase is organized as the Missouri Territory.

1814 British major William McKay and his troops capture the American fort at Prairie du Chien, Wisconsin, only one month after it is built; it is the only military confrontation to date in that area of the Northwest Territory.

1815 Unaware that a peace treaty has been signed, British troops unsuccessfully attack 4,500 Americans (mostly Tennessee and Kentucky frontiersmen) near New Orleans.

A TIMELINE OF MAJOR EVENTS

PART I *1816–1836 Moving the Frontier West*

UNITED STATES HISTORY

1816 James Monroe is elected the fifth president of the United States.

1817 The New York State legislature grants $7 million for the building of the Erie Canal.

1820 The fourth census of the U.S. cites the nation's population at 10 million.

Taking the census

1823 President Monroe presents his Monroe Doctrine to Congress, warning European nations not to interfere in the internal affairs of countries in the Western Hemisphere.

1824 John Quincy Adams is elected president by the U. S. House of Representatives when no other candidate wins a majority vote in the national election.

1825 The Erie Canal is completed; it runs from Lake Erie to the Hudson River at Albany, New York.

1826 Thomas Jefferson and John Adams die on the same day—July 4, 1826.

1828 Andrew Jackson becomes the seventh president of the U.S., defeating John Quincy Adams.

1830s Under the Indian Removal Act of 1830, thousands of Cherokee, Seminole, Choctaw, Creek, and Chickasaw Indians are moved from their homes in Alabama, Tennessee, Georgia, and Mississippi to Oklahoma, in what is known as the Trail of Tears; 4,000 die en route.

1830 The nation's first regular steam railway service, with twenty-three

THE CONQUEST OF THE WEST

1816 Indiana is admitted as the nineteenth state of the Union.

1818 The U.S. and Britain sign an agreement fixing the northern boundary of the U.S. at the 49th parallel, from the Great Lakes to the Rocky Mountains. The agreement allows both nations to settle in Oregon for ten years.
•Illinois becomes the twenty-first state.

1819 Controversy erupts over the Missouri Territory's petition for statehood. Its entry to the Union will upset the balance between free and slave states.
•The U.S. and Spain sign the Adams-Onis Treaty. Spain gives up eastern Florida and its claim to the Pacific Northwest, while the U.S. recognizes Spain's claim to Texas.
•Alabama becomes the nation's twenty-second state.

1820 The Missouri Compromise is passed by Congress. Missouri is admitted as a slave state, Maine as a free state, and slavery is illegal in all Western territory north of latitude 36' 30".
•With the permission of the Mexican government, Americans begin settling in the Mexican province of Texas.

Map of the Missouri Compromise

1825 Congress declares much of what are now the states of Kansas and Oklahoma to be a permanent Indian frontier; the land is thought to be worthless for settlement.

miles of track, is opened to the public by the South Carolina Canal and Rail Road Company.
•Daniel Webster and Robert Hayne hold a ten-day-long senatorial debate over the issues of national union vs. states rights.

1831 Cyrus McCormick, an American inventor, develops the reaper, revolutionizing farming in the United States and the world.

1832 Nominated by the newly formed Democratic Party, Andrew Jackson is reelected president of the U.S.

1833 The *New York Sun*, the first successful daily newspaper, is founded; an issue costs one penny.

1834 Abraham Lincoln enters politics for the first time, joining the assembly of the Illinois legislature; he is twenty-five years old.

1835 The national debt is completely paid off through revenues from increased railroad construction and land values.
•An assassination attempt is made against President Jackson by Richard Lawrence, who claims that he is the rightful heir to the English throne.
•The Second Seminole War begins in Florida when the U.S. government asks the Seminoles to give up their reservation.

1836 Martin Van Buren is elected president of the United States.

The Webster-Hayne Debate

1827 The U.S. and Britain renew the 1818 "joint occupation" agreement on Oregon.

1830 Mexico refuses to allow more Americans to settle in Texas and bans slavery in the region.
•According to the 1830 census, more than 3.5 million people—a fourth of the nation's population—live in Western states and territories.

1832 The Battle of Velasco, in South Texas, is the first incident of bloodshed between Texans and Mexicans.

The Alamo

1833 American settlers in Texas vote to secede from Mexico. Clashes between American settlers and Mexican authorities in Texas increase.

1836 An army under Mexican President López de Santa Anna surrounds about 180 Texan rebels in the Alamo, a mission church. The Alamo is captured, and all its defenders are killed, on March 6.
•Over 300 Texans captured at Goliad are killed by Santa Anna's troops on March 27.
•Sam Houston, commander of the Texan Republic's army, defeats Santa Anna at San Jacinto on April 21, winning independence for Texas.
•Arkansas is admitted as the twenty-fifth state.

SETTLING THE WESTERN CLAIMS

Before the business of settling the West could begin, it was necessary to determine who had rights to those lands between the Appalachian Mountains and the Mississippi River.

The charters of the original thirteen colonies often left Western boundaries unfixed. When almost all the nation's citizens lived on or near the East Coast, such borders were unimportant. But as pioneers moved west of the Appalachians, important questions arose. Who would govern the new "overmountain" settlements? What was their relationship with the original states and the new government?

Most important was the question of state claims. Nearly all the states claimed "outlets" or "reserves" of Western land. (Connecticut, for example, claimed a strip of land in what is now Ohio, which is still known as the Western Reserve.)

In the early 1780s, states began to give their Western claims over to the national government. The question of how these lands would be divided among settlers remained. With the Land Ordinance of 1785, Congress established a uniform system for the sale of public land in the West. The government surveyed its new holdings and divided them up into "townships," each six miles square. The townships were divided into thirty-six square-mile lots, which were finally divided into smaller units available to settlers at a minimum of $1 an acre. The ordinance also specified that one lot in each township would be used to pay for public schools.

In 1794, in the region that became Indiana, General Anthony Wayne (1745—96; above) defeated an Indian force at the Battle of Fallen Timbers. The Treaty of Greenville, signed the following year between local Indians and white authorities, secured the region for white settlement.

While the states ceded their land claims peacefully, the land's inhabitants—the American Indians—often resisted attempts to settle on their homelands. However, treaties signed with the Iroquois and several other Indian nations in 1784 at Fort Stanwix, and at Fort Harmar (opposite, top) in 1785, helped clear the way for white settlement west of the Appalachian Mountains.

This 1797 map (opposite, bottom) shows the large area claimed as "Western Territory" by Georgia. A year after the map's publication, this territory was ceded to the federal government and organized as the Mississippi Territory.

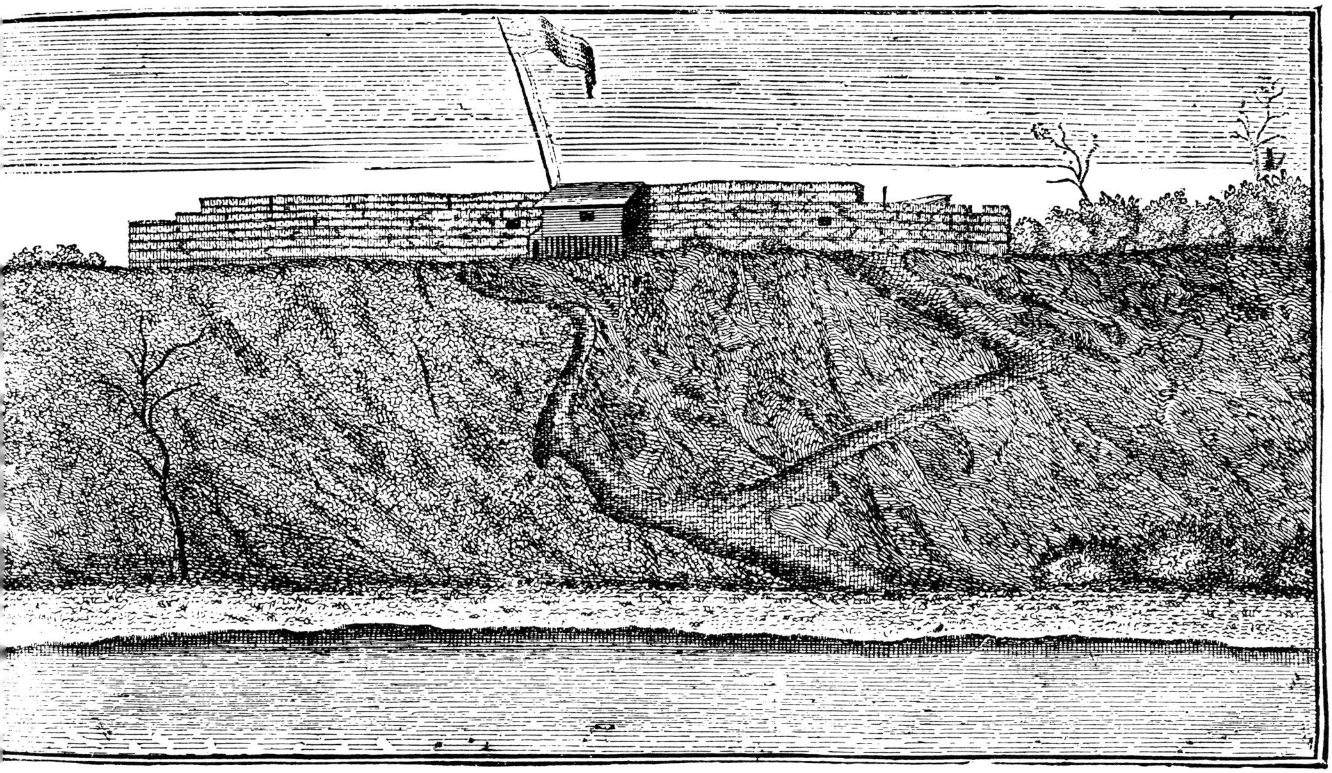

MAP of the Southern Parts of the UNITED STATES OF AMERICA By Abraham Bradley jun.
PART OF KENTUCKY
PART OF VIRGINIA
TENNESSEE
NORTH CAROLINA
SOUTH CAROLINA
GEORGIA
GEORGIA WESTERN TERRITORY
WEST FLORIDA
EAST FLORIDA
Scale
C.H. Court House
Longitude calculated from Washington
Drawn & Engraved for Morse's American Gazetteer

THE OLD NORTHWEST

One of the first Western regions to be settled was the land bordered by the Great Lakes to the north, the Mississippi River to the west, and the Ohio River to the south—the Northwest Territory.

The Land Ordinance of 1785 determined how Western lands would be surveyed and sold, but hadn't specified how the lands would be divided or governed, or whether they would become actual states equal to the original thirteen. The result was the Northwest Ordinance, based on the recommendations of Thomas Jefferson (1743–1826).

Adopted by Congress in July 1787, the ordinance called for the eventual creation of no less than three and no more than five states from the Northwest Territory. It also stated that these new states would be "on an equal footing with the original states in all respects whatever." Initially, Congress would govern the territory. When its population reached 5,000 voting citizens (which in those days meant free white men), it could elect a legislature and send a nonvoting representative to Congress. When any part of the territory had 60,000 voting citizens, it could apply to become a state. The ordinance also prohibited slavery in the Northwest Territory.

The Northwest Ordinance set a political pattern followed by most other new states over the next 125 years. Eventually, five states—Illinois, Indiana, Michigan, Ohio, and Wisconsin—were created from the "Old Northwest."

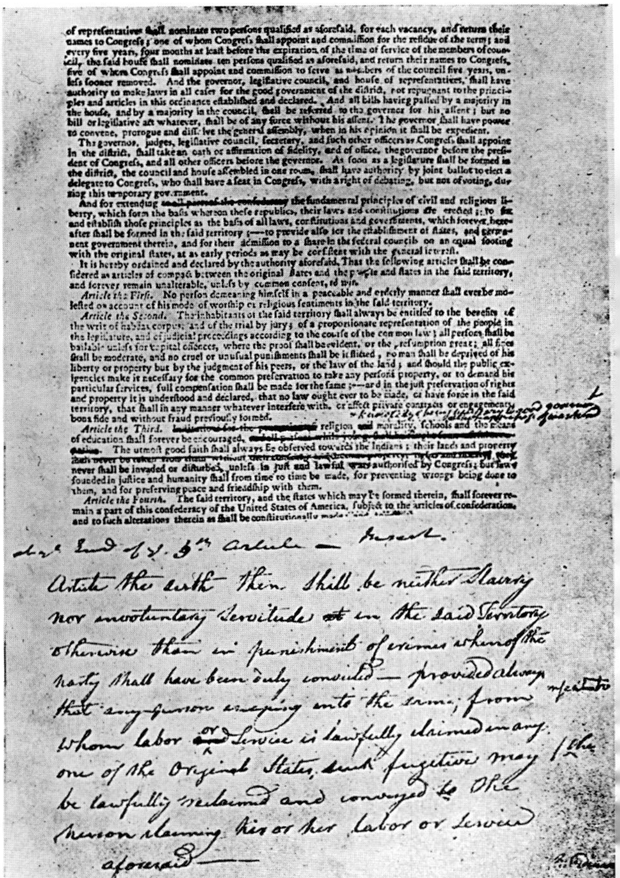

of representatives shall nominate two persons qualified as aforesaid, for each vacancy, and return their names to Congress; one of whom Congress shall appoint and commission for the residue of the term; and every five years, four months at least before the expiration of the time of service of the members of council, the said house shall nominate ten persons qualified as aforesaid, and return their names to Congress, five of whom Congress shall appoint and commission to serve as members of the council five years, unless sooner removed. And the governor, legislative council, and house of representatives, shall have authority to make laws in all cases for the good government of the district, not repugnant to the principles and articles in this ordinance established and declared. And all bills having passed by a majority in the house, and by a majority in the council, shall be referred to the governor for his assent; but no bill or legislative act whatever, shall be of any force without his assent. The governor shall have power to convene, prorogue and dissolve the general assembly, when in his opinion it shall be expedient.

The governor, judges, legislative council, secretary, and such other officers as Congress shall appoint in the district, shall take an oath or affirmation of fidelity, and of office, the governor before the president of Congress, and all other officers before the governor. As soon as a legislature shall be formed in the district, the council and house assembled in one room, shall have authority by joint ballot to elect a delegate to Congress, who shall have a seat in Congress, with a right of debating, but not of voting, during this temporary government.

And for extending the fundamental principles of civil and religious liberty, which form the basis whereon these republics, their laws and constitutions are erected; to fix and establish those principles as the basis of all laws, constitutions and governments, which forever hereafter shall be formed in the said territory;—to provide also for the establishment of states, and permanent government therein, and for their admission to a share in the federal councils on an equal footing with the original states, at as early periods as may be consistent with the general interest.

It is hereby ordained and declared by the authority aforesaid, That the following articles shall be considered as articles of compact between the original states and the people and states in the said territory, and forever remain unalterable, unless by common consent, to wit.

Article the First. No person demeaning himself in a peaceable and orderly manner shall ever be molested on account of his mode of worship or religious sentiments in the said territory.

Article the Second. The inhabitants of the said territory shall always be entitled to the benefits of the writ of habeas corpus, and of the trial by jury; of a proportionate representation of the people in the legislature, and of judicial proceedings according to the course of the common law; all persons shall be bailable unless for capital offences, where the proof shall be evident, or the presumption great; all fines shall be moderate, and no cruel or unusual punishments shall be inflicted, no man shall be deprived of his liberty or property but by the judgment of his peers, or the law of the land; and should the public exigencies make it necessary for the common preservation to take any persons property, or to demand his particular services, full compensation shall be made for the same;—and in the just preservation of rights and property it is understood and declared, that no law ought ever to be made, or have force in the said territory, that shall in any manner whatever interfere with, or affect private contracts or engagements, bona fide and without fraud previously formed.

Article the Third. [illegible] religion, morality, schools and the means of education shall forever be encouraged, [illegible] The utmost good faith shall always be observed towards the Indians; their lands and property [illegible] never shall be invaded or disturbed, unless in just and lawful wars authorised by Congress; but laws founded in justice and humanity shall from time to time be made, for preventing wrongs being done to them, and for preserving peace and friendship with them.

Article the Fourth. The said territory, and the states which may be formed therein, shall forever remain a part of this confederacy of the United States of America, subject to the articles of confederation, and to such alterations therein as shall be constitutionally made [illegible]

[illegible] Article — Insert.

Article the sixth There shall be neither Slavery nor involuntary Servitude in the said Territory otherwise than in punishment of crimes whereof the party shall have been duly convicted — provided always that any person escaping into the same, from whom labor or Service is lawfully claimed in any one of the Original States, such fugitive may be lawfully reclaimed and conveyed to the person claiming his or her labor or service aforesaid —

Although a slaveowner himself, Thomas Jefferson didn't want slavery to spread to the West. In 1784, his proposal to forbid slavery in all Western territories after 1800 was defeated by one vote. Jefferson succeeded in getting an antislavery clause included in the Northwest Ordinance of 1787. This draft printing of the Northwest Ordinance (above) contains handwritten notes by Nathan Dane, a leading settler in what would become Indiana. In 1800, Indiana became the first territory to be organized by Congress from the "Old Northwest."

This map "of the north west parts of the United States" (right) was published in 1785, the same year that Congress passed the important Land Ordinance establishing how Western lands were to be surveyed and divided.

The first major settlement in Ohio, Marietta (named for Queen Marie Antoinette of France), was founded in 1788 at the meeting place of the Muskingum and Ohio rivers. In this nineteenth-century engraving (below), settlers listen as Congress's proclamation of territorial government for Ohio is read aloud.

FROM THE APPALACHIANS TO THE MISSISSIPPI

Settlers from the Southern colonies began moving into the lands west of the Appalachians even before the Revolutionary War. By 1775, there were permanent settlements in what local Indians called "the dark and bloody ground"—the region that became Kentucky, the nation's fifteenth state, in 1792.

After the Revolutionary War, pioneers arrived in territory claimed by North Carolina along the Tennessee River. In 1784, settlers proclaimed the region the "State of Franklin" and named John Sevier (1745–1815) as governor. Franklin lasted four years before North Carolina regained control of the territory. Parts of Franklin were incorporated into the new state of Tennessee in 1796.

South of Kentucky and Tennessee, and west to the Mississippi River, lay still more land for settlement. However, settlement here was slow in coming because of conflicts with the region's Indians and Spain's control of Florida, which then included much of the coast of the Gulf of Mexico. (Spain finally ceded Florida to the United States in 1821.) From this region came the states of Mississippi (admitted in 1817) and Alabama (1819).

General James Wilkinson (1757–1825) and former vice president Aaron Burr (1756-36; above) were involved in a still-mysterious conspiracy to set up an "empire" in the West, to be ruled either by themselves or with the help of Spain. The scheme failed when Wilkinson betrayed Burr, and Burr was barely acquitted of treason.

This 1851 lithograph (above) portrays an incident, probably legendary, that supposedly took place near Fort Henry (present-day Wheeling, West Virginia) in 1777. According to the legend, Major Samuel McCulloch was ambushed by Indians while bringing news of an Indian attack on the fort. He was forced to leap (on horseback) 150 feet into Wheeling Creek to escape.

This nineteenth-century painting by Frederic Remington (right) depicts pioneers from Virginia moving across the Blue Ridge Mountains into Kentucky before the Revolutionary War. Kentucky and Tennessee were the first Western lands to attract many permanent white settlers.

THE HISPANIC WEST

Much of the American West originally belonged to Spain. From the sixteenth to the eighteenth century, Spanish soldiers, explorers, and missionaries pushed north from Mexico, establishing a chain of outposts and religious missions from the coast of California to the deserts of Arizona. But Spanish rule didn't always go unchallenged. In the early 1680s, for example, Hopi Indians in Arizona rebelled against their Spanish rulers and briefly threw them out of the region.

As Spain's status as a world power declined, so did its control over its American possessions. In 1810, the first of a series of revolts broke out in Mexico. Eleven years later Mexico won independence from Spain and took control of Spain's North American colonies, including California, New Mexico, and Texas.

But Mexico's control over its northern provinces soon began to slip. The turmoil that followed Mexican independence led some settlers in regions like California to wonder if their provinces wouldn't be better off as independent states. Also, some of Mexico's territories, especially California and New Mexico, had established commercial ties with the United States. The stage was set for a conflict between two young nations—Mexico and the United States—for the control of a great portion of the North American West.

One of the great figures of Spain's New World colonization was Junípero Serra (1713–84), a Franciscan friar. In the 1760s and 1770s, Serra helped found several outposts in California that strengthened Spain's control of the region. This engraving of Serra (above) appeared in a 1787 book published in Mexico City.

Spain built a chain of missions—combined churches, schools, and government outposts—in California. The missions taught local Indians European farming methods and crafts. Shown here (opposite, top) is the Mission of St. Louis, built in 1798, as it looked in 1840.

This French lithograph (opposite, bottom), published in 1780, shows the Spanish presidio (fort) guarding the small California town that eventually became the city of San Francisco.

THE WEST COAST

At the start of the nineteenth century, five nations (Britain, France, Russia, Spain, and the United States) claimed the Oregon Country—the Pacific Northwest, including what is now Washington and Oregon.

America's claim to the territory began in 1792, when Captain Robert Gray (1755–1806) reached the area and discovered the mouth of a great river he later named for his ship, the *Columbia*. (Lewis and Clark explored the area more than a decade later.) In 1811, traders commissioned by John Jacob Astor (1763–1848), then the richest man in America, arrived in Oregon as part of Astor's plan for a fur-trading empire to be called "Astoria." The first Astoria expedition ended in disaster when its ship blew up.

By the early 1800s, France, Russia, and Spain had largely given up their claims to the Oregon Country, leaving Britain and the United States to compete for the region. In 1818, the two nations signed a treaty that settled the border between American and British (later Canadian) territory at the 49th parallel from the Great Lakes to the Rocky Mountains. Because neither nation could agree on the Oregon Country's exact borders, the region was put under "joint occupation," an arrangement that lasted for the next twenty-five years.

Russia became active in the region that is now the state of Alaska during the seventeenth century. By the 1800s, Russian outposts had spread south along the Pacific Coast into northern California. Shown here (above) is the Russian trading post on Bodega Bay, just north of San Francisco, in 1821.

This page from the logbook of Captain Robert Gray's ship Columbia *(opposite) describes the vessel's arrival off the coast of the Oregon Country in 1791. After discovering the Columbia River, Gray sailed on to the Orient, finally returning to Boston with a cargo of Chinese tea and silk.*

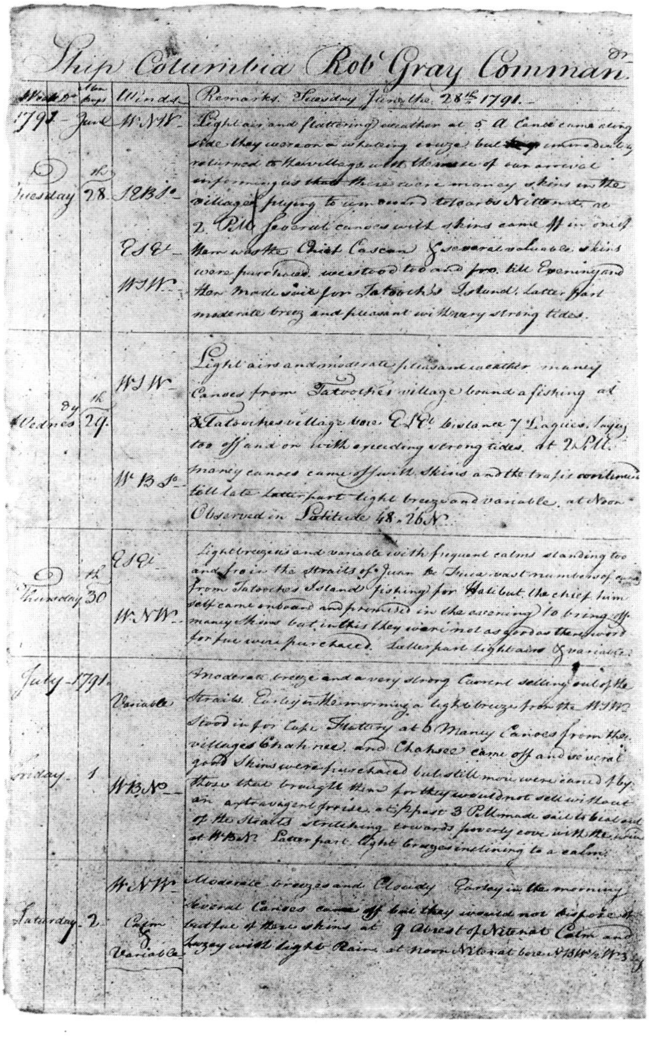

Ship Columbia Robt Gray Commander

Week Days	Month Days	Winds	Remarks Tuesday June the 28th 1791.
1791 Tuesday	June 28th	W N W, S B S, E S E, W S W	Light airs and flattering weather at 5 A Canoe came along side they were on a whaling cruze but immediately returned to the village with the news of our arrival informing us that there were many skins in the village plying to windward towards Nittenat at 2 PM several canoes with skins came off in one of them was the Chief Cascan & several valuable skins were purchased we stood too and fro till Evening and then made sail for Tatooche's Island. Latter part moderate breez and pleasant with very strong tides.
Wednesday	29th	W S W, W B S	Light airs and moderate pleasant weather many Canoes from Tatooche's village bound a fishing at [illegible] Tatooche's village bore E S E distance 7 Leagues, laying too off and on with exceeding strong tides. at 2 PM many canoes came off with skins and the trafic continued till late. Latter part light breezes and variable. at Noon Observed in Latitude 48.26 N.
Thursday	30th	E S E, W N W	Light breezes and variable with frequent calms standing too and fro in the Straits of Juan de Fuca vast numbers of canoes from Tatooche's Island fishing for Halibut the chief him self came onboard and promised in the evening to bring off many skins but in this they were not as good as their word for few were purchased. Latter part light airs & variable.
July 1791 Friday	1	Variable, W B N	A moderate breeze and a very strong Current setting out of the Straits. Early in the morning a light breeze from the W N W. Stood in for Cape Flattery at 6 Many Canoes from the villages Chahnee and Chahsee came off and several good Skins were purchased but still more were carried by those that brought them for they would not sell without an extravagent price. at ½ past 3 PM made sail to beat out of the Straits stretching towards poverty cove with the wind at W B N. Latter part light breezes inclining to a calm.
Saturday	2	W N W, Calm & Variable	Moderate breezes and Cloudy Early in the morning several Canoes came off but they would not dispose of but few of their skins at 9 Abrest of Nitenat Calm and hazey with light Rain at Noon Nitenat bore N B W ½ W 3 [illegible]

THE LOUISIANA PURCHASE

Like the Oregon Country, the vast area beyond the Mississippi River was a source of conflict. From the earliest days after its discovery, North America had often been a pawn in European power politics. This did not change with the Revolutionary War. The young United States shared the continent with Great Britain to the north and Spain to the south and west. France had lost most of its influence after defeat in the French and Indian War of 1754–63, but in 1800, it again appeared on the scene.

The region known as Louisiana—a huge territory stretching from the Mississippi River west to the Rocky Mountains and north to Canada—belonged to France until 1762, when it passed to Spain. In 1800, French ruler Napoleon Bonaparte (1769–1821) persuaded Spain to return Louisiana to France in the Treaty of San Ildefonso.

The treaty was a secret, but the change in ownership became known two years later, when Spanish authorities forbade American traders to use the port of New Orleans. (Spain still governed the area, despite the change in ownership.) Americans—including President Thomas Jefferson—quickly became anxious. Napoleon's desire to gain an empire in the Americas to match the one he was building in Europe was well known. With Louisiana in French hands, the United States would have a possibly hostile foreign nation controlling its western border, the Mississippi River, and New Orleans.

When Juan Ventura Morales, the Spanish Intendant (governor) of New Orleans, refused to allow American merchants to store goods at the port—a "right of deposit" guaranteed by a 1795 treaty—President Thomas Jefferson (above) began the diplomatic effort that resulted in the Louisiana Purchase.

New Orleans, capital of Louisiana, was founded by the French explorer Jean Baptiste le Moyne, Sieur de Bienville, in 1717. Here he and his men are depicted surveying the area (below). New Orleans's location at the mouth of the Mississippi River soon made it one of the most important cities in North America.

NEGOTIATING THE LOUISIANA PURCHASE

France's newest enterprise in North America quickly ran into trouble. In 1801, revolt broke out on France's Caribbean island colony of Haiti. The bloody conflict that followed gave Napoleon second thoughts about his plan for an American empire. Also, war with Britain seemed likely, which would leave the French government with little money and few troops to spend on an American adventure.

The idea that the United States might seize the opportunity to buy Louisiana from France took time to develop. At first, President Jefferson wanted only to reopen New Orleans to American trade. He instructed the United States minister to France, Robert Livingston (1746–1813), to start negotiations with French foreign diplomats as soon as possible. Next, he authorized Livingston (later joined by James Monroe, 1758–1831) to offer to buy New Orleans, along with West Florida, for no more than $10 million.

Livingston and Monroe, much closer to the French political scene than Jefferson back in Washington, realized that France might be willing to sell all of Louisiana, not just New Orleans. They made an unauthorized offer to buy the territory for about $15 million—and in April 1803 the French government accepted their offer.

In 1776, Robert Livingston (above) helped Thomas Jefferson draft the Declaration of Independence. Twenty-five years later Jefferson, now president, appointed Livingston U.S. minister to France, where he led the negotiations for the Louisiana Purchase.

This lithograph (above) shows Robert Livingston (left) and James Monroe (center) discussing the borders of the Louisiana Territory with the wily French statesman Charles Maurice de Talleyrand. Talleyrand advised Napoleon Bonaparte to reject the American offer to purchase Louisiana—advice the French ruler ignored.

A NATION REDOUBLED

Livingston and Monroe's deal with France put President Jefferson in an awkward position. His political philosophy did not include ideas of territorial expansion, and he wasn't even sure the Constitution gave him the authority to approve the purchase.

But the Louisiana Territory was simply too great a bargain to pass up, and Jefferson threw his support behind the deal, which the Senate eagerly ratified. On October 20, 1803, the Louisiana Purchase passed into law. A month later the United States took possession of New Orleans. France handed over the rest of the purchase on December 20. In early 1804, Congress organized the region into the Territory of Orleans (roughly the current state of Louisiana) and the Territory of Louisiana.

The United States had doubled its size practically overnight for a final cost of about 4 cents an acre. No one knew the exact extent of the Louisiana Territory (its vague borders would be a source of controversy for years), but it included about 800,000 square miles. All or part of fifteen states eventually came from the Louisiana Territory.

In 1803, Jefferson appointed his secretary Meriwether Lewis and army officer William Clark to lead an exploring expedition through the Louisiana Territory. The expedition left St. Louis in early 1804, reached the West Coast in the summer of 1805, and returned to St. Louis the following year. This woodcut (below) shows the two explorers meeting with Indians.

"WAR HAWKS" OF THE WEST

The congressional elections of 1810 brought a new breed of politicians to Washington. They were dubbed the "war hawks" because of their aggressive attitude toward the European powers who still controlled much of North America—Spain and Britain.

The war hawks belonged mostly to the Democratic-Republican party and came chiefly from the West and the newer Southern states. Congressmen from both regions wanted the United States to expand its territory, even at the risk of war. Those from the West, who included Senator Henry Clay (1777–1852) and Kentucky Representative Richard Johnson (1780–1850), hoped to add Canada to the United States. Those from the South, led by South Carolina senator John C. Calhoun (1782–1850), wanted to seize Florida from Spain. Support for the war hawks' policy was especially great in the Northwest Territory. This region suffered from Indian conflicts that settlers believed were inspired by British authorities in Canada.

The war hawks were opposed by congressmen of the Federalist party, most of whom represented the New England states. They wanted to avoid a conflict with Britain, which they knew would hurt the already weakened trade-based economies of their home states. But in 1812, despite frantic diplomatic maneuvering by President James Madison and the British government, Great Britain and the United States went to war.

Henry Clay's attacks on Britain helped bring about the War of 1812, but Clay (above) also served on the commission that negotiated peace with Britain in 1814. Back in Congress, Clay promoted what he called the "American System"—a series of economic measures aimed at strengthening the ties between the Eastern United States and the West.

Clashes with Indians on the northwestern frontier grew worse in 1811. In late November of that year, Governor William Henry Harrison of Indiana and his 1,000 troops were ambushed along Tippecanoe Creek by Indians under the Shawnee leader Tenskwatawa. Harrison routed the Indians after a fierce battle, but the raids continued. This diagram (opposite, bottom) shows Harrison's camp before the battle.

Thomas Hart Benton of Missouri (right) spent much of his three decades in the Senate promoting Western expansion. Benton was a fighter personally as well as politically: In 1813, he and his brother Jesse tangled with Andrew Jackson in a tavern brawl. Benton later became a firm friend and supporter of Jackson's.

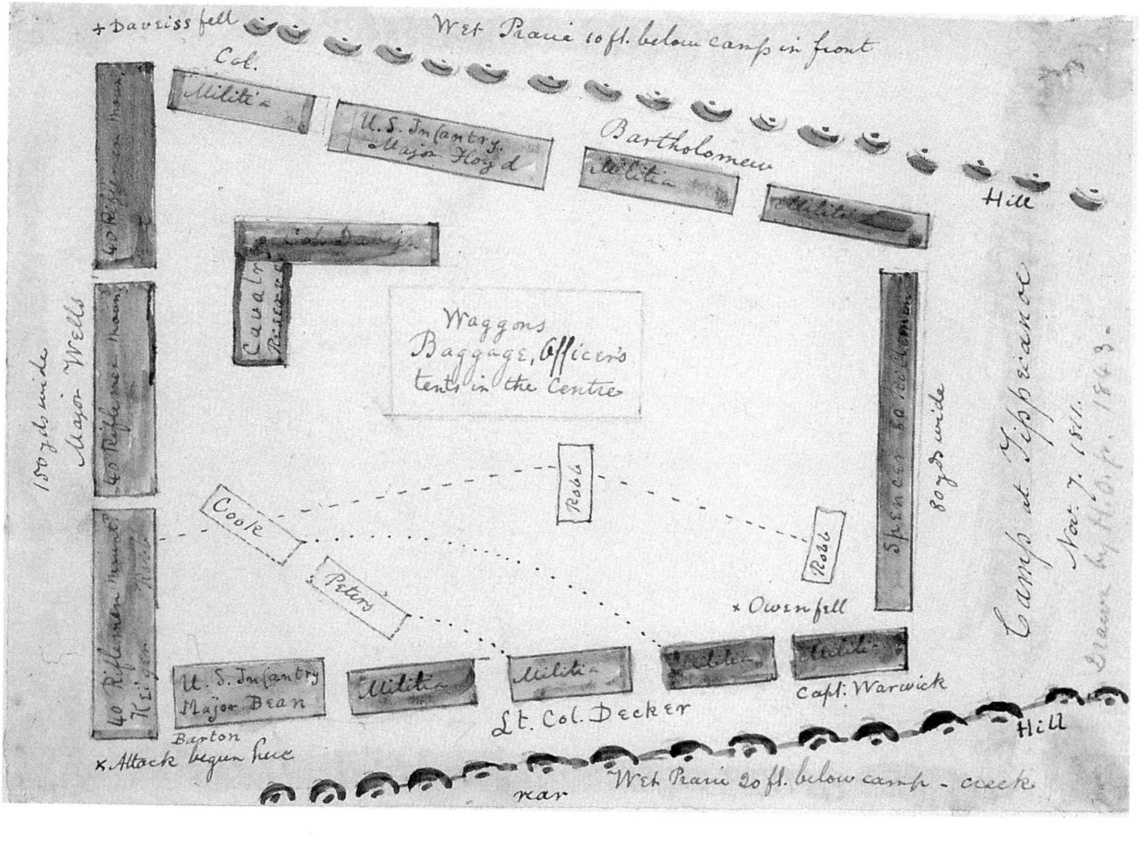

THE WAR OF 1812

Western politicians had been the loudest supporters of a war with Britain, but the best-known battles of the War of 1812 were fought on the border between New York and Canada, on the Great Lakes, or at sea. The West also saw its share of fighting.

On July 12, 1812, American general William Hull (1783–1825) led 2,000 men into Canada from Michigan. But in early August, Hull retreated back into American territory, fearing the British and their Indian allies would be too much for his force. Hull finally surrendered his base, Fort Detroit, to the British on August 16. By that time, two American forts in the Northwest Territory—Fort Dearborn, near the site of present-day Chicago, and Fort Michilimackinac, on an island in Lake Michigan—had already fallen.

The war on the frontier took a turn for the better in 1813. In May of that year, General William Henry Harrison (1773–1841) fought off a British attack on Fort Meigs in Ohio. In October, Harrison defeated a British and Indian force along the Thames River in what is now Ontario, Canada. Tecumseh (1768–1813), the great Shawnee Indian leader, died in the battle. The war reached farther west to Oregon, where the British occupied the American fur-trading post, Astoria, in November.

In December 1814, Great Britain and the United States signed a peace treaty in Ghent, Belgium. But one more battle remained.

TECUMSEH.

Together with his brother Tenskwatawa (sometimes called "Prophet" or "Shawnee Prophet"), the Shawnee Indian leader Tecumseh (above) traveled throughout the West in an attempt to form an Indian confederacy to halt white settlement. During the War of 1812 Tecumseh became a general in the British army.

General Henry Dearborn (1751–1829; right) was the U.S. Army's highest-ranking officer at the start of the War of 1812. Given the job of defending the northwest frontier, Dearborn presided over several humiliating defeats and was finally removed from command by President James Madison.

Fort Detroit, one of the major American bases on the northwest frontier, was originally a French outpost, as indicated by the notes accompanying this 1764 map (below). The map clearly shows how close the fort was to the British territory just across the Detroit River.

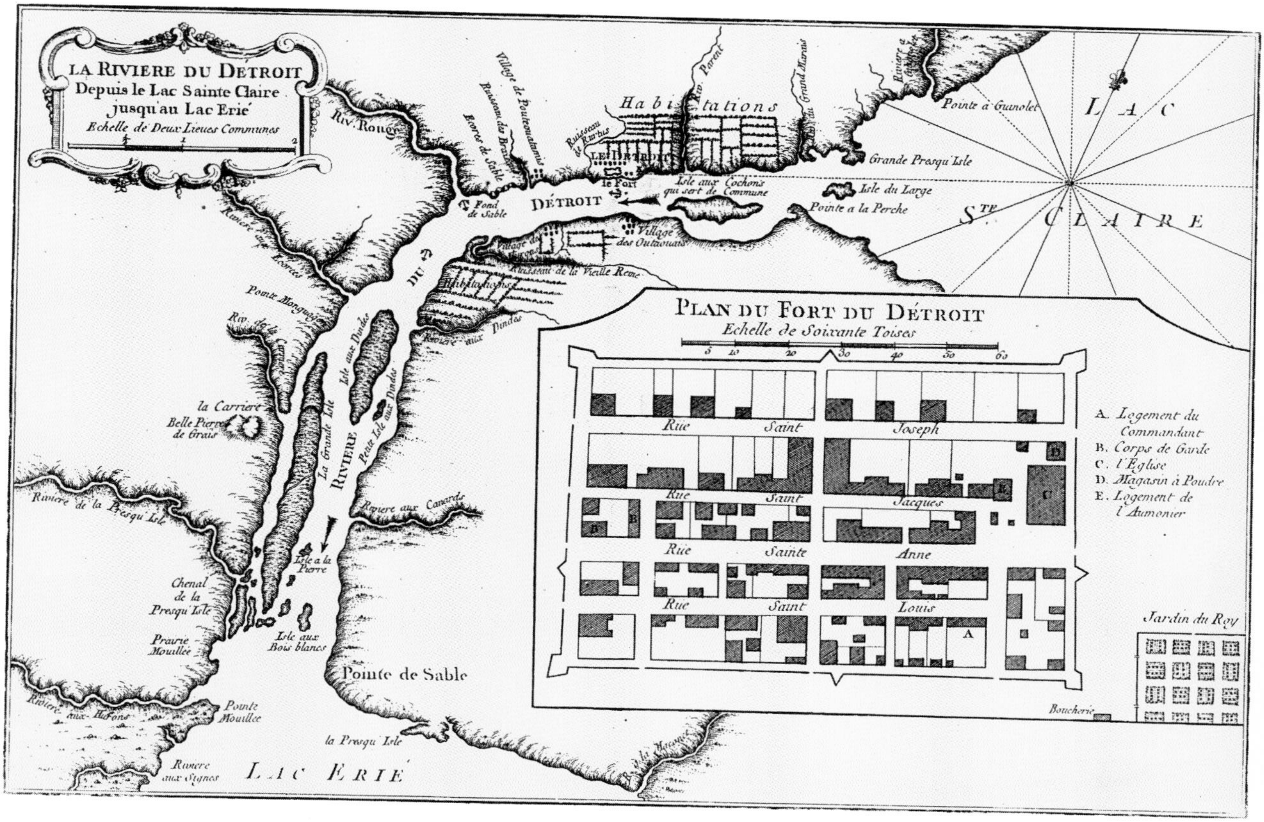

THE BATTLE OF NEW ORLEANS

In the fall of 1814, Britain planned to end its war with the United States with one major operation. War with France had prevented Britain from sending a major force to America. But now that Napoleon had been defeated at Waterloo, a British army commanded by Sir Edward Pakenham (1778–1815) headed to America intending to capture New Orleans.

The American commander in the area, General Andrew Jackson (1767–1845), assembled 6,000 men, mostly Western frontiersmen, to defend the city against 7,500 veteran British troops.

Pakenham landed his men in the swamps near New Orleans after defeating a tiny American fleet. On the morning of January 8, he ordered his red-coated soldiers forward against American positions.

The result was a slaughter. Firing from cover, the Americans killed or wounded about 2,000 British in less than an hour—including Pakenham, who was mortally wounded. The British quickly retreated. The American losses totaled seventeen killed and forty-five wounded. With the victory at New Orleans, American control of the Mississippi Valley was secure, and the nation had a new hero, Andrew Jackson.

It was a brilliant, but unnecessary, American victory. A peace treaty had been signed two weeks before the battle. But because of the slow pace at which news traveled in the early nineteenth century, neither side knew about it.

General Andrew Jackson's victory over the British at the Battle of New Orleans in January 1815 inspired many popular songs and poems. This image (above) is the cover of a piano piece celebrating the battle.

Andrew Jackson (right) developed a lifelong hatred of the British when he became a prisoner of war during the American Revolution at age thirteen. His toughness during a campaign against the Creek Indians of Alabama in 1813–14 won him the nickname "Old Hickory." Jackson's success against the Indians led to his appointment as a major general.

Unlike the British, who formed for the attack in neat lines, the Americans at the Battle of New Orleans (below) crouched behind bales of cotton for cover. Also, many of New Orleans's defenders used long-barreled "Kentucky rifles," which were far more accurate than the smoothbore muskets carried by the British regulars.

"FIREBELL IN THE NIGHT"

In 1817, the Missouri Territory, organized five years earlier from part of the Louisiana Purchase, asked Congress for statehood. A fierce political battle quickly broke out.

The source of the controversy was slavery. Many Northerners hoped it would be forbidden in Missouri and other Western territories, but many Southerners hoped it would survive.

Congress first considered the issue in 1817, without reaching a decision. In 1819, it came up again. By that time, the Alabama Territory had been admitted as a slave state. Now the question was not only moral but political: admitting Missouri as a slave state would upset the balance between free and slave states in Congress.

Senator Henry Clay of Kentucky helped draft a set of laws known as the Missouri Compromise. Maine would be admitted as a free state and Missouri as a slave state, preserving balance in Congress. But the compromise prohibited slavery in the area north of latitude 36' 30"—Missouri's southern border. The measures were finally adopted in 1820.

The Missouri Compromise solved one small part of the slavery problem. But it didn't resolve the larger issue, something former president Thomas Jefferson realized. In a letter to a friend, Jefferson wrote of the compromise: "This momentous question . . . like a firebell in the night awakened and filled me with terror. I considered it the knell of the Union."

Abolitionists (people who wanted slavery completely ended, or abolished) faced violence and even death for their beliefs. After the Missouri Compromise, editor Elijah Lovejoy had to move his antislavery newspaper to the free state of Illinois. Even in Illinois, however, there was much support for slavery. Lovejoy was finally killed in an attack, shown in this woodcut (below), by a proslavery mob on November 7, 1837.

"GONE TO TEXAS"

The vast territory that eventually became the state of Texas was first explored and colonized by Spain. Texas became a Mexican province when Mexico won its independence from Spain in 1821.

American interest in Texas began after the Louisiana Purchase in 1803. Some Americans felt that the vaguely defined purchase included part of Texas, although the U.S. government did not press the claim. A handful of Americans settled in Texas in the first years of the nineteenth century.

In 1820, Moses Austin (1721–1861) of Missouri asked Mexican authorities for land and permission to found an American settlement in Texas. It was granted, but Austin died soon afterward. The Mexican government allowed his son, Stephen (1793–1836), to settle no more than 300 American families in Texas, but these 300 were just the beginning of a great wave of American emigration to Texas. By 1836, there were 50,000 Americans in the region.

Conflict between American Texans and the Mexican government broke out almost immediately. The Americans were supposed to obey Mexican laws and convert to Roman Catholicism, but most did neither. Also, Mexico had outlawed slavery, but American settlers in Texas, many of them from the South, brought slaves with them. American Texans, in turn, resented the attempts of the distant Mexican government to control their new homeland.

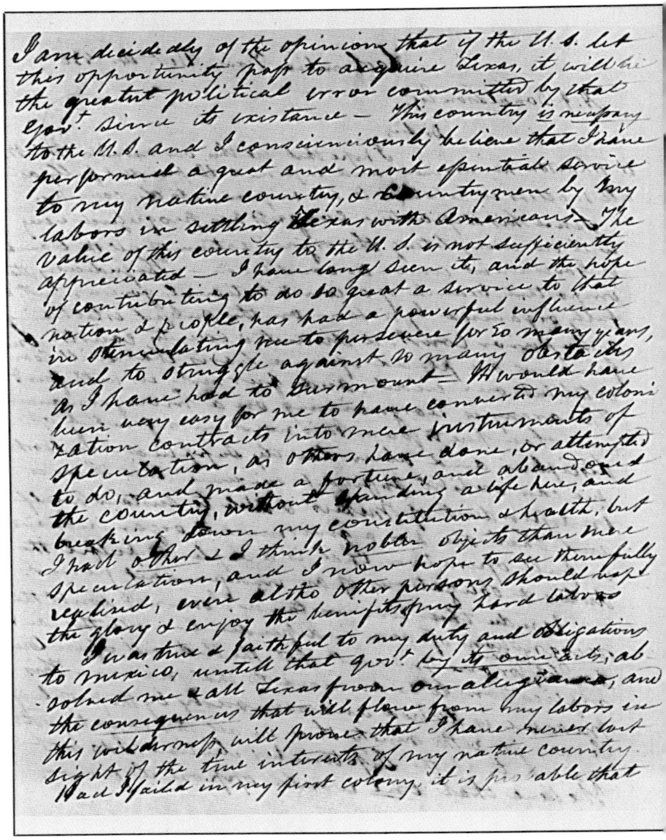
I am decidedly of the opinion that if the U.S. let this opportunity pass to acquire Texas, it will be the greatest political error committed by that govt. since its existance — This country is necessary to the U.S. and I conscienciously believe that I have performed a great and most essential service to my native country, & countrymen by my labors in settling Texas with Americans — The value of this country to the U.S. is not sufficiently appreciated — I have long seen it, and the hope of contributing to do so great a service to that nation & people, has had a powerful influence in stimulating me to persevere for so many years, and to struggle against so many obstacles as I have had to surmount — It would have been very easy for me to have converted my colonization contracts into mere instruments of speculation, as others have done, or attempted to do, and made a fortune, and abandoned the country, without spending a life here, and breaking down my constitution & health, but I had other & I think nobler objects than mere speculation, and I now hope to see them fully realized, even altho other persons should reap the glory & enjoy the benefits of my hard labors

I was true & faithful to my duty and obligations to Mexico, untill that govt. by its own acts, absolved me & all Texas from our allegiance, and the consequences that will flow from my labors in this wilderness will prove that I have never lost sight of the true interests of my native country. Had I failed in my first colony, it is probable that

Most American emigrants to Texas wanted the region to become part of the United States. That feeling is reflected in this letter (above), written by Stephen Austin in December 1836, following Texas's successful revolt against Mexico. The letter states the belief held by Austin (then Texas's secretary of state) that an American refusal to annex Texas would be "the greatest political error committed by that [government] since its existence."

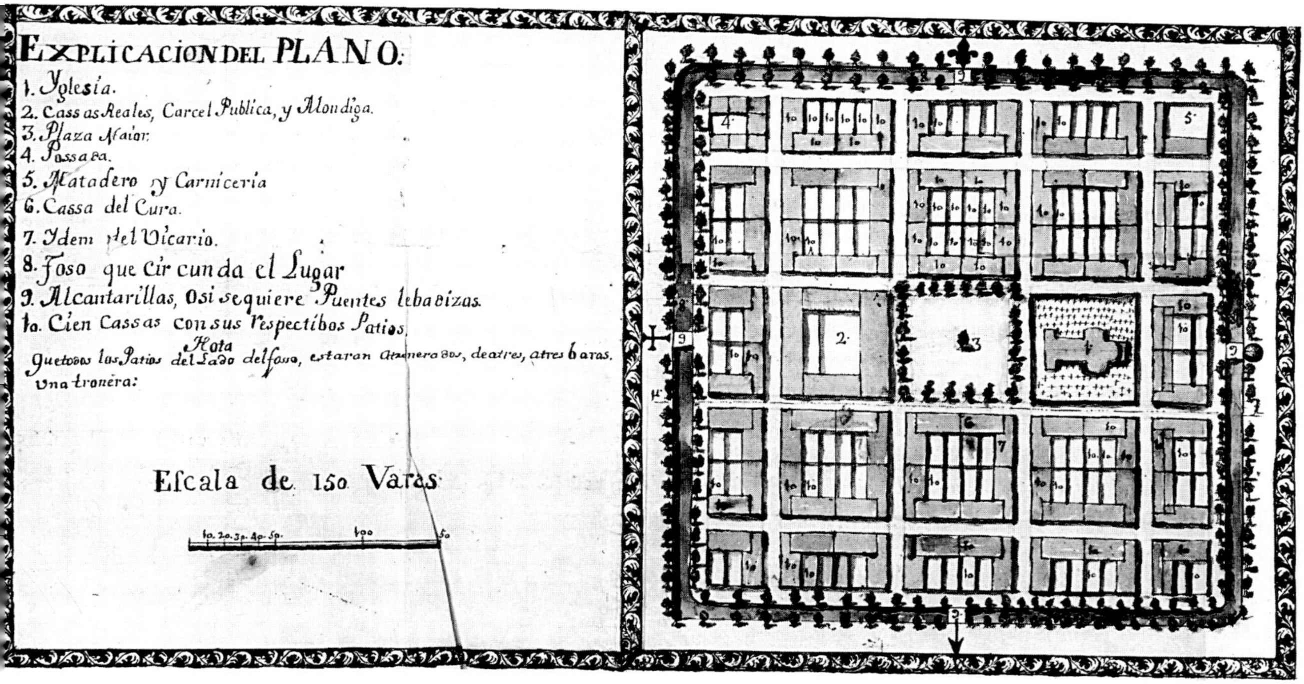

Explicacion del Plano:
1. Yglesia.
2. Cassas Reales, Carcel Publica, y Alondiga.
3. Plaza Maior.
5. Matadero y Carniceria
6. Cassa del Cura.
7. Idem del Vicario.
8. Foso que circunda el Lugar
9. Alcantarillas, o si se quiere Puentes lebadizos.
10. Cien Cassas con sus respectibos Patios.
Escala de 150 Varas

San Antonio (above), founded in 1718, was Spain's (and later Mexico's) chief outpost in the region that became Texas. Like most Spanish colonial towns, San Antonio was laid out around a central square, or plaza, as shown in this 1780 diagram.

Stephen Austin (right) led 300 families to Texas to settle on the land granted to his father, Moses, by the Mexican government.

Part II: 1837–1849
Manifest Destiny Fulfilled

The first great territorial gain for the United States, the Louisiana Purchase, came about through diplomacy, not through war. But as more and more Americans moved west, tensions arose between the United States and the other powers in North America—Great Britain and Mexico. Britain and the United States both claimed the Oregon Country, which they governed together for twenty-five years. By the 1840s, however, American demand for all of Oregon grew louder. In 1846, a compromise with Britain gave much of the Oregon Country to the United States in order to avoid war.

Unfortunately, conflict with Mexico wasn't resolved as peacefully. In 1836, American settlers in the Mexican province of Texas rebelled and, in a brief but bloody war, won independence as the Republic of Texas. A decade later the United States annexed Texas, and within a few months the United States and Mexico were at war.

Historians are divided in their opinions of what caused the Mexican War, but most agree that it was largely fought to win territory from Mexico. If this was the case, the United States achieved a stunning but hard-fought victory. After defeating the Mexican army on the battlefield, the United States won practically all of Mexico's northern territories, including California. Americans who spoke of "Manifest Destiny"—the idea that it was the United States' God-given right to expand across the entire North American continent—saw their dreams fulfilled. The United States now stretched from the Atlantic to the Pacific.

In this Currier & Ives lithograph, General Winfield Scott rides into the main square of Mexico City. Scott's genius for planning and carrying out complex operations had paid off in a great victory for the United States. In the words of the Duke of Wellington, "His campaign was unsurpassed in military annals."

A TIMELINE OF MAJOR EVENTS

PART II *1837-1849 Manifest Destiny Fulfilled*

UNITED STATES HISTORY

1837 The Panic of 1837, caused by large state debts and previous land speculation, begins; many people move westward in search of work.

1838 Representative John Quincy Adams introduces 350 petitions against slavery into the House of Representatives.
•A proslavery mob burns down the new meeting house of the Philadelphia Female Anti-Slavery Society.
•The House of Representatives adopts a new "gag rule," prohibiting any discussion of the issue of slavery.

1839 The Aroostook War, a land conflict involving Maine and New Brunswick, Canada, ends without bloodshed when American general Winfield Scott arranges a truce with New Brunswick.
•The Whig National Convention nominates William Henry Harrison for president.

1840 William Henry Harrison defeats Martin Van Buren in the presidential elections using the campaign slogan "Tippecanoe and Tyler, too." John Tyler is elected vice president.

1841 President Harrison dies after only one month in office. John Tyler succeeds him.
•Tyler vetoes a Whig-sponsored bank bill and his entire cabinet, except Secretary of State Daniel Webster, resigns.

1842 The Second Seminole War, in

Harrison and Tyler campaign poster

THE CONQUEST OF THE WEST

1837 Michigan becomes the twenty-sixth state.
•President Andrew Jackson recognizes the Republic of Texas as a nation. Most of the 30,000 citizens of Texas want it to be part of the U.S.

1838 The Iowa Territory is organized. It includes most of the land that is now the states of Iowa, Minnesota, and North and South Dakota.

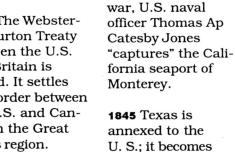

1842 The Webster-Ashburton Treaty between the U.S. and Britain is signed. It settles the border between the U.S. and Canada in the Great Lakes region.
•Mistakenly thinking that the U.S. and Mexico are at war, U.S. naval officer Thomas Ap Catesby Jones "captures" the California seaport of Monterey.

1845 Texas is annexed to the U. S.; it becomes the twenty-eighth state in 1846.

1846 In April, U.S. and Mexican forces clash along the Rio Grande; General Taylor's troops defeat a Mexican force at Palo Alto in the first major battle of the war. The U.S. declares war on Mexico on May 11.
•American settlers in California declare their independence as the "Bear Flag Republic."
•The "Oregon Question" is resolved. The U.S. and Britain agree to end the joint occupation of the region and divide

The Battle of Palo Alto

which U.S. troops destroy the crops of Flordia's Seminole Indians and force them to sign a peace treaty which relocates them to eastern Oklahoma, ends after a five-year conflict.

•The U.S. Supreme Court rules in *Prigg v. Commonwealth of Pennsylvania* that owners may recover escaped slaves, although states do not have to assist them.

1843 Daniel Webster resigns as secretary of state.

1844 President Tyler appoints John Calhoun secretary of state.

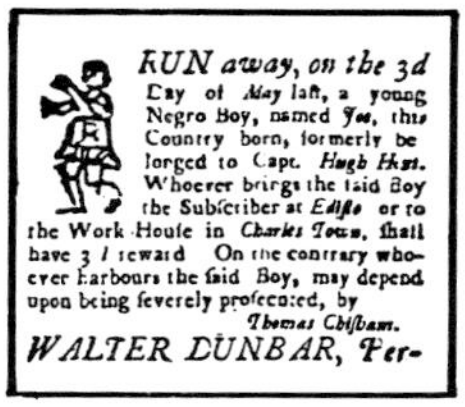
RUN away, on the 3d Day of May last, a young Negro Boy, named Joe, this Country born, formerly belonged to Capt. Hugh Hext. Whoever brings the said Boy the Subscriber at Edisto or to the Work-House in Charles Town, shall have 3 l reward. On the contrary whoever harbours the said Boy, may depend upon being severely prosecuted, by

Thomas Chisham.

WALTER DUNBAR, Per-

A notice of a runaway slave

•James Polk defeats Henry Clay for the presidency. James Birney of the Liberty Party wins 62,300 popular votes and is a vital factor in Clay's defeat.

1848 A coalition of antislavery groups forms the Free Soil party and nominate Martin Van Buren for president.

•The Whigs nominate General Zachary Taylor for president. He wins the election with Millard Fillmore as his vice president.

•The first Women's Rights Convention meets at Seneca Falls, New York; the participants demand equal education and the right to vote.

1849 Congress establishes the U.S. Department of the Interior.

•The Gold Rush begins as the first gold miners arrive in San Francisco aboard the ship *California*.

•Author Henry David Thoreau publishes *Civil Disobedience*, an essay he wrote while in jail for refusing to pay taxes that would have supported the Mexican War effort.

The Battle of Monterrey

the territory at the 49th parallel.

•Taylor's army captures the Mexican city of Monterrey in September. The U.S. "Army of the Desert," commanded by Colonel Stephen W. Kearny, reaches California. On the way, Kearny proclaims U.S. rule over New Mexico.

1847 After a short truce, Taylor inflicts another defeat on the Mexican Army at Buena Vista in February.

•General Scott takes command from Taylor.

•Scott's troops land near the Mexican port city of Veracruz in March. After a siege, the city surrenders.

•Scott and 9,000 men reach Mexico City. After fighting at Molino del Rey and Chapultepec Castle, the Americans capture the city.

1848 The United States and Mexico sign the treaty of Guadelupe-Hidalgo. In return for about $18 million, Mexico surrenders the present-day states of California, New Mexico, Arizona, Colorado, Nevada, and Utah.

•Wisconsin becomes the thirtieth state; it is declared a free state.

•Oregon is officially organized as a territory. It becomes a free state in 1859.

1849 Mormon settlers organize the "State of Deseret" in what later becomes Utah.

THE IDEA OF MANIFEST DESTINY

The July 1845 edition of New York's *Democratic Review* contained an editorial by John L. O'Sullivan. Written specifically to support the U.S. annexation of Texas, O'Sullivan's article introduced a phrase that was eagerly adopted by supporters of Western expansion—"Manifest Destiny."

"It is our manifest destiny," wrote O'Sullivan, "to overspread the continent allotted by Providence for the free development of our yearly multiplying millions."

As the nation approached the middle of the nineteenth century, enthusiasm for territorial expansion ran high. Supporters of Manifest Destiny argued that more Western land was needed to provide space for the new Americans created by a high birth rate and increased immigration. They pointed out that lands governed by Mexico and Britain were sparsely populated and mostly unproductive. Why should these lands be left to their "inefficient" owners when "industrious" American settlers could put them to better use?

Of America's two major political parties, the Democrats and the Whigs, the Democrats were the more vocal supporters of Western expansion. In the presidential election of 1836, Democratic candidate James K. Polk (1795–1849) defeated his Whig rival, Henry Clay. Polk would serve only one term, but his four years in office did much to put the philosophy of Manifest Destiny into action.

Horace Greeley (1811–72; above), editor of the influential New York Tribune, *is often credited with urging Americans to support Manifest Destiny by writing "Go West, young man, and grow up with the country" in an 1865 editorial. The phrase had actually been used in 1851 by the* Terre Haute (*Indiana*) Express.

This cartoon (opposite, top), published in the early months of President James Polk's administration, makes fun of several political controversies of the time—including the Oregon Question. The ragtag band of "brave soldiers" in the left foreground shows the cartoonist's opinion that the United States was ill-equipped to back up its claim to Oregon with force.

One group that pushed west in the era of Manifest Destiny was the Mormons, members of a religious sect founded in New York State in 1830. After being driven out of Illinois in 1846, about 30,000 Mormon settlers traveled overland to settle the land that became the state of Utah. This engraving (opposite, bottom) shows Mormon emigrants in the Rocky Mountains.

Empire Club!
Plaze yer honor's worship, can't ye do somethin' for me? I was borr-n in Boston and rared in New-Yorrk, be the howly St Patrick, and nivver a bit of an office have I had yet.
Can't you do something for us? we are poor weak women in great danger of being seduced! We want a proclamation in behalf of our Moral Reform Society.
That's right Jemmy, Non Committal. By the Eternal you're a chip of the old block.
Let this Poke manage two stools if he can, I'll cut my stick, and be off for the sunny south.
Go to Texas!
Dod rot this administration! I've lost my sittivation that Tyler give me, that was worth $15 a year! Dod rot 'em, I say!
Why you see sir I was an Officer with Govr. Dorr, and I should like to be an Officer agin: But I aint perticklar, if you haint got no office may be you've got some old Clothes to give me!
What Office do you expect, my man?
Calhoun
Polk
For Oregon!! Liberty! or Death!!!
I'll be the Organ
No you wont!
Madisonian
Follow me brave soldiers, strike but one blow, and Oregon is ours!
Buchanan.
Jones
Globe
Blair.

THE TEXAN REVOLUTION: THE ALAMO AND GOLIAD

While not all Eastern settlers in Texas wanted immediate independence from Mexico, many hoped for eventual liberation. But Mexico was under the dictatorial rule of President López de Santa Anna (1795–1876), who had no intention of negotiating a peaceful solution to the problem.

The Texan Revolution began in October 1835, when American rebels took over the towns of Gonzales and San Antonio. On March 2, 1836, they declared Texas an independent republic and chose Sam Houston (1793–1863), formerly of Tennessee, to lead the republic's tiny army.

By then, Santa Anna was on his way to San Antonio with several thousand troops. He laid siege to the Alamo, a small mission church in San Antonio. The Alamo was defended by 187 rebels, including such famous Western figures as Davy Crockett (1786–1836) and James Bowie (1796–1836).

The Alamo finally fell on March 6. Despite the many legends associated with the Alamo, few details of the attack are known for certain. None of the defenders lived through the final assault; survivors may have been executed after the battle. The fall of the Alamo was followed by an even worse defeat a week later, when 400 rebels were captured and killed at the town of Goliad. By the beginning of April, the Texan Revolution seemed on the edge of collapse.

James Bowie (left) was another famous Western figure who joined the Texan Revolution and died at the Alamo. Bowie is credited with inventing the long-bladed knife that bears his name, but the actual inventor may have been his brother Rezin.

This woodcut (right) shows famous frontiersman (and former Tennessee congressman) Davy Crockett killing a Mexican officer with the butt of his rifle during the battle for the Alamo. This incident, like many associated with the siege, has more basis in legend than in fact.

Mexican troops launch their final assault on the Alamo in this 1885 painting (below). Estimates of the number of Mexican forces vary, but Santa Anna probably commanded between 2,000 and 4,000 men during the siege. Fewer than 200 Texans defended the Alamo.

SAN JACINTO AND INDEPENDENCE

The defeats at Goliad and the Alamo left Sam Houston with a force of less than 400 men, which he led in a retreat to the Brazos River. The government of the new Republic of Texas fled to Galveston Island.

Houston was retreating but not running away from the fight. Within a few weeks, new Texan volunteers doubled the army's size. Santa Anna, thinking the revolt had been crushed, split his larger Mexican army into smaller units—a decision that proved to be disastrous for Mexico. On April 20, the Texans reached the San Jacinto River, where they found Santa Anna. The next day, after destroying a bridge to make retreat impossible for the Mexicans, the Texans attacked.

Houston's men had the element of surprise, and they overwhelmed Santa Anna and his troops in twenty minutes. Accounts of what happened next are not clear, but the Texans killed hundreds of Mexican prisoners in revenge for the Alamo and Goliad. Santa Anna himself was captured on April 22 and was forced to order his remaining troops back into Mexico.

Houston's victory at San Jacinto made Texan independence a fact. The Mexican government refused to acknowledge the loss of its province, but the Texans had made it clear that military force could not bring it back under Mexican rule.

In this cartoon (above), Mexican generals López de Santa Anna and Martín de Cos offer their swords to Texan general Sam Houston while denying responsibility for the massacres at the Alamo and Goliad. Houston's Indian clothing may be a reference to the years he spent living with the Cherokee Indians of Tennessee as a young man.

ANNEXATION

In October 1836, the Republic of Texas set up a constitution, a new president (Sam Houston), and an elected government to replace the provisional one organized in March. The United States and the European powers immediately recognized the new nation.

The Houston government, along with many Texans, hoped for annexation by the United States. But it was not forthcoming. Northern congressmen opposed it because they knew that Texas would ask for admission as a slave state. They also feared that Texas might be admitted not as one large state but as several smaller ones, again upsetting the balance between free and slave states in Congress.

Mirabeau Lamar (1798–1859) succeeded Houston as president in 1838. The Lamar government was more concerned with solving Texas's many internal problems—including a growing national debt and conflict between east and west Texas—than with annexation. In 1841, Houston returned to the presidency and renewed the movement for annexation. The matter came to a head in 1845. Mexico, under diplomatic pressure from Britain and France, was now ready to recognize Texas's independence, while Congress had finally offered annexation. The Texan government had to make a choice: continued independence or annexation by the United States.

Annexation won. In December 1845, Texas became the twenty-eighth state of the Union, with slavery allowed.

This 1844 cartoon (opposite, top), titled "Texas Coming In," shows the reactions of several American political figures to the proposal to annex Texas to the United States. Sam Houston and Stephen Austin, riding in a boat labeled "Texas," are greeted by Democratic presidential candidate James K. Polk. Meanwhile, politicians opposed to annexation, led by Whig candidate Henry Clay, try to pull the boat away from American soil.

Cockfighting (combat between specially trained roosters) was a popular sport in nineteenth-century America. This cartoon (opposite, bottom), "Clay and Polk in the Texan Annexation Cockpit," depicts the two candidates fighting out the question of Texas's annexation as their supporters cheer from the sidelines.

All hail to James K. Polk, the friend of our Country!
TEXAS
Welcome Texas! welcome brothers.
Polk.
Oh evil day, that ever I got into the footsteps of my predecessor.
If we let go, we are ruined, and if we hold on— Oh! crackee!
Clay
Webster
Garrison.
Abolition.
SALT RIVER
Frelinghuysen
Curse the day that ever I got hold of this rope! this is a bad place to let go of it— But I must!
Avaunt! unholy man! I will not keep company with a blackleg.
H. Bucholzer

I'll bet one of my best Chowders on the Kentucky Rooster.
Cock a doodle doo doo.
They rejected me, let them look to their Champion!
By the Eternal! I doubt the pluck of that Cock from Tenessee, if he does go for Texas.

THE MEXICAN WAR: BACKGROUND TO CONFLICT

When Democratic president James K. Polk took office in 1845, he made no secret of his expansionist views. At first, Polk seemed more interested in Oregon than in Mexico's northern lands, but he and his supporters also had their eyes on California. Political turmoil in Mexico further complicated the situation.

Tensions between the United States and Mexico had been rising years before the first shots of the Mexican War were fired. The most obvious strain between the two nations was over the Republic of Texas. Mexico had never really acknowledged Texas's independence. In 1843, Mexican ruler López de Santa Anna stated that annexation of Texas would be "equivalent to a declaration of war."

There were other causes for conflict, too. Polk sent diplomatic missions to Mexico in an effort to resolve some of the disagreements between the two nations, especially over the exact border between Mexico and Texas. All failed. Military force replaced diplomatic efforts in early 1846, when Polk ordered General Zachary Taylor (1784–1850) to lead an American army into the disputed area between the Rio Grande and the Nueces River in Texas. Polk probably hoped Taylor's presence would provoke a Mexican attack, thus giving the United States the chance to declare war and seize Mexico's vast Western lands.

Although he won the Democratic presidential nomination in the election of 1844, former Tennessee governor James Knox Polk (opposite, top) was so little known nationally that Whigs chanted "Who is James Polk?" at campaign rallies. But the United States gained more territory during his single term than in any other except Thomas Jefferson's.

President Polk sent diplomat John Slidell (opposite, bottom) to Mexico in September 1845, with an offer to buy California and New Mexico. The Mexican government's refusal even to listen to Slidell's proposal was one of the factors that led Polk to order U.S. troops to Texas in early 1846.

The outbreak of the Mexican War caused bitterness in New England (where many saw the conflict as a war to add new lands for slavery) and joy in the South and West, where support for Manifest Destiny was strongest. This painting, "News of the War" (below), shows residents of a small town reading news of the first battles in Mexico and California.

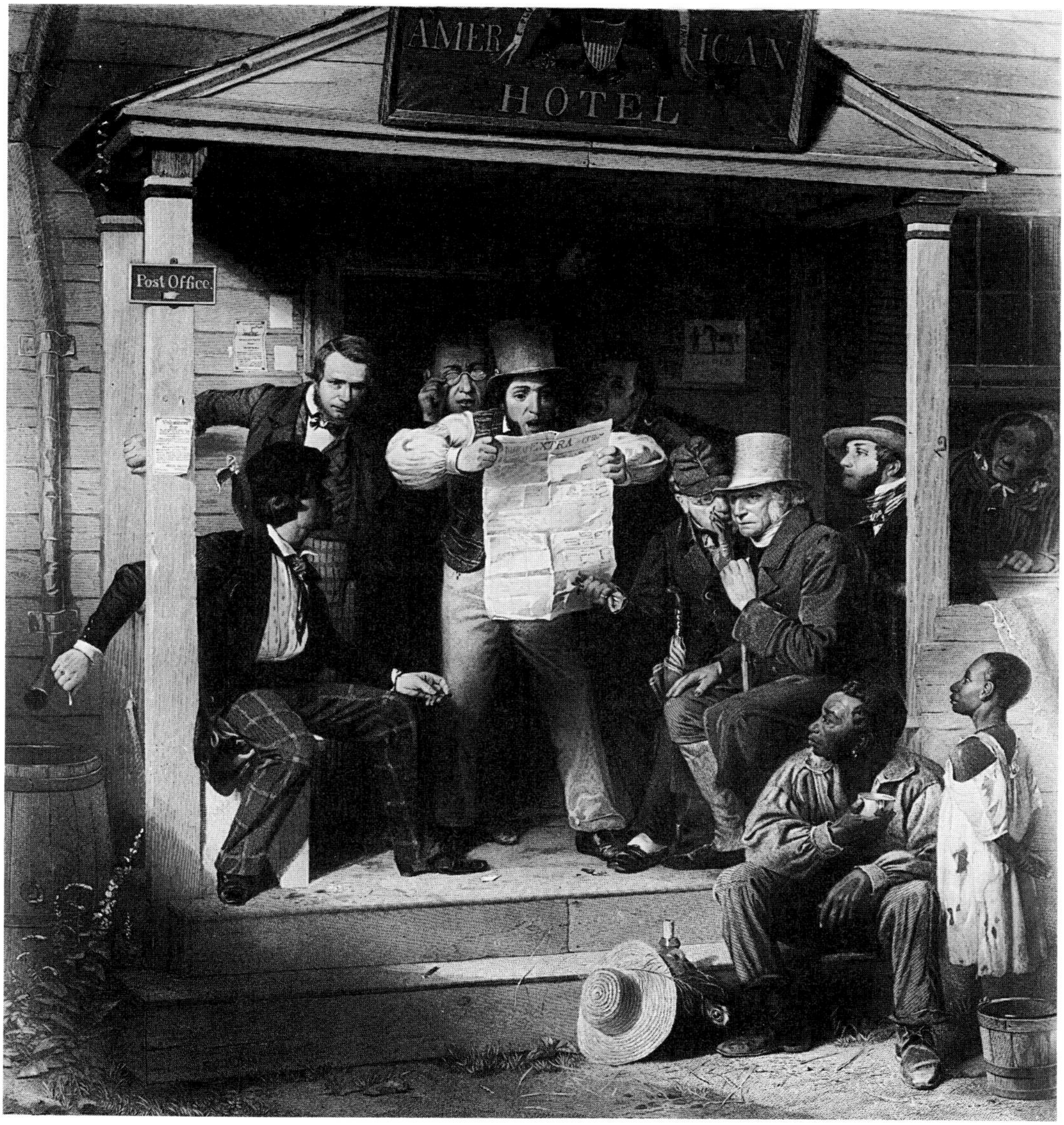

PALO ALTO TO BUENA VISTA

In the spring of 1846, two armies warily watched each other from opposite sides of the Rio Grande River. On the north was Zachary Taylor's American "Army of Observation." South of the river was a far larger Mexican force. In April, the Mexicans asked Taylor to withdraw his troops. When Taylor refused, Mexican General Mariano Arista (1802–55) sent a cavalry unit across the Rio Grande. The Mexicans ran into an American patrol on April 24, and eleven Americans were killed in the skirmish that followed.

News of the fighting reached Washington two weeks later. On May 11, Polk told Congress, "Mexico . . . has shed American blood on American soil" and asked for a declaration of war. By that time, Taylor's army had already fought its first major battles on Mexican soil. On May 8, Mexican forces attacked Taylor at a watering hole called Palo Alto, and the fighting continued at nearby Resaca de la Palma. The Americans won both battles.

Taylor led his troops deeper into Mexico. In September, after capturing the city of Monterrey, Taylor negotiated a truce with the Mexican commanders—which President Polk revoked. In February, a Mexican force under López de Santa Anna attacked Taylor at Buena Vista. After fierce fighting, with heavy casualties on both sides, the American positions held. Buena Vista was the last major battle of the war in northern Mexico.

General Zachary Taylor sits calmly astride his horse, Old Whitey, as the Battle of Palo Alto rages around him (above). Taylor's informal style—despite his splendid appearance in this lithograph, he rarely wore a uniform— earned him the nickname "Old Rough and Ready."

One of the fiercest battles in Mexico was the American assault on Monterrey (below), a heavily fortified town defended by 10,000 Mexican troops. After capturing the roads surrounding Monterrey, Taylor's men stormed into the city on September 22, 1846, where they fought hand-to-hand and house-to-house with Mexican troops, as shown in this lithograph.

Santa Anna led 20,000 Mexican soldiers against the American army at Buena Vista, outside Saltillo, on February 22, 1847. The Americans were forced to retreat on the first day of battle, but on February 23 they recaptured the positions they had lost in a headlong charge (above). The Mexicans broke off the battle and retreated south that night.

THE BEAR FLAG REPUBLIC

By the 1840s, many Americans were interested in the fertile lands of California. As in Texas, Mexico had difficulty maintaining its authority over the sparsely populated region, and many of its residents (including a few American settlers) had come to resent having a distant government in Mexico City. President Polk tried to take advantage of this dissatisfaction by offering to buy the lands of California and New Mexico in 1845, but the Mexican government turned him down.

In June 1846, some American settlers declared independence from Mexico and proclaimed California the "Bear Flag Republic." The name came from their first crude flag. John C. Frémont (1813–90), an American army officer leading an exploring expedition through the area, was named leader of the republic, which quickly voted to join the United States.

In the summer of 1846, American naval forces landed at Monterey, San Francisco, and other coastal towns. But the United States didn't take California without a fight. In September, shortly after Commodore Robert F. Stockton (1795–1866) reported "peace and harmony" in California, Mexican-Californians revolted against American rule. The rebellion drove American forces from the towns they had occupied. But in January 1847, American reinforcements arrived overland to complete the conquest of California.

This poster (from the election of 1856; right) portrays John C. Frémont as a brave explorer. Frémont had been nicknamed "The Pathfinder" for his three mapping expeditions as an army officer in the West, but his political ambitions (inspired partly by his father-in-law, Senator Thomas Hart Benton) often interfered with his military duties.

San Diego, California, had a population of about 500 when a force commanded by John C. Frémont captured it in July 1846. Later it was occupied by General Stephen Kearny's "Army of the West." This engraving (below) shows the American flag flying over the town, which one of Kearny's soldiers called "a few adobe houses."

THE SOUTHWEST CAMPAIGNS

The conquest of New Mexico (the land between Texas and California) was another goal of the United States in the Mexican War. That assignment was given to General Stephen W. Kearny (1794–1848). In July 1846, Kearny and about 2,000 troops left Fort Leavenworth for Santa Fe, the region's capital. Kearny's small "Army of the West" captured the town without a fight.

As in California, early conquest gave way to rebellion. In January 1847, New Mexicans in Taos killed the territory's American-appointed governor and began a revolt. The uprising was brutally put down in February. By that time, Kearny had reached California and helped end the rebellion there.

Two other units won distinction in the Southwest. The first was a regiment of volunteer horsemen from Missouri led by Alexander Doniphan (1808–87). Doniphan's troops advanced into the northern Mexican state of Chihuahua in December 1846, and they won several battles against Mexican troops.

The "Mormon Battalion," a unit recruited from Mormon settlers in what would later become Utah, performed a similar feat. The Mormons were ordered to march to California from Utah by way of Santa Fe. Five hundred survivors reached San Diego in January 1847. The Mormons saw no combat, but the fierce desert terrain they had to cross was as dangerous as any human enemy.

General Stephen Watts Kearny (right) conquered New Mexico and led an army overland to California in a brilliant campaign, only to become embroiled in a political dispute between John C. Frémont and Commodore Robert Stockton. Kearny was finally named governor of California in 1848.

The capture of Chihuahua City in northern Mexico was a goal of Alexander Doniphan's Missouri volunteers. But to get there, they had to cross the Sacramento River, which was guarded by a large Mexican force. In the battle depicted here (below), fought on February 28, 1847, Doniphan's troops inflicted a severe defeat on the Mexicans.

VERACRUZ TO CHURUBUSCO

General Zachary Taylor's success in northern Mexico made him an enemy of President Polk. Polk feared the popular general would be a potential rival in the 1848 presidential election. At the end of 1847, Polk assigned most of Taylor's troops to General Winfield Scott (1786–1866).

Scott aimed at nothing less than the capture of Mexico City, the nation's capital. In its first major amphibious operation, the U.S. Navy landed Scott and 12,000 troops near the Mexican port of Veracruz on March 10, 1847. The navy shelled Veracruz into surrender by March 28.

Scott had to act quickly. Many of his troops were volunteers whose short terms of enlistment would soon end. Also, the dreaded disease called yellow fever would appear with hot weather; the Americans could escape the disease only by leaving the swampy coast. (Throughout the war, disease killed far more American soldiers than did Mexican bullets.) Scott set out for Mexico City in early April, following the same route that Spanish *conquistador* Hernán Cortés had traveled four centuries earlier.

The Americans reached Churubusco, a few miles from Mexico City, in mid-August. Along the way the army fought battles at Cerro Gordo, Puebla, and Contreras. On August 20, they managed to drive back an attack by Santa Anna. Scott granted the Mexicans a truce, but peace talks quickly broke off. More fighting lay ahead.

One of the major victories of Scott's campaign was Cerro Gordo, where Santa Anna was nearly captured. The Mexican leader left behind a chest of gold and, according to some accounts, his wooden leg. In this cartoon (above), General Scott offers Santa Anna "a hasty plate of soup" from the Mexican leader's own carriage.

Sea power played a major role in General Winfield Scott's campaign in central Mexico. Here Commodore David Conner's squadron shells the fortifications guarding Veracruz (opposite, top). After the capture of the city, Conner's ships blockaded the Gulf of Mexico to prevent much-needed military supplies from reaching Santa Anna's army.

This Currier & Ives lithograph (opposite, bottom) shows Mexican troops abandoning San Juan de Ulua, Veracruz's chief fort, while their officers surrender the city to General Winfield Scott. Scott's artillerymen were aided by sailors who brought huge naval guns ashore to strengthen the American bombardment of the fort and city.

THE FALL OF MEXICO CITY

"Scott is lost!" exclaimed the Duke of Wellington (1769–1852), the foremost British general of the time, when he heard that the American army had left Veracruz to advance on Mexico City by land. Few European generals believed the outnumbered Americans would ever reach the capital. But they did, though battles and Mexican guerrilla attacks took a heavy toll in casualties. Scott's success was due both to the bravery of his troops and the skill of his West Point–trained officers. Many of these young soldiers—like captains Ulysses S. Grant and Robert E. Lee and Colonel Jefferson Davis—later held high military and political rank on both sides in the Civil War.

Two major obstacles blocked the way into Mexico City: Molino del Rey, a cannon factory, and Chapultepec Castle, Mexico's military academy. An American attack captured Molino del Rey on September 8, 1847. Four days later, after a bombardment with American artillery, Scott's troops, led by a detachment of marines, charged Chapultepec Castle. The Mexican defenders—including teenage cadets—fought heroically, but Chapultepec fell.

On September 14, after final street fighting, General Scott rode into Mexico City's plaza and watched the American flag go up over the National Palace. The shooting had ended, but a peace treaty still had to be negotiated before the Mexican War could end.

This lithograph, which is highly inaccurate like most contemporary views of Mexican War battles, depicts the storming of Chapultepec Castle. In fact, the Americans had to use ladders to clamber up the castle's steep sides. Also, the Americans never fought in the full-dress uniforms shown here.

THE TREATY OF GUADALUPE HIDALGO

In early 1847, President Polk charged American diplomat Nicholas Trist (1800–74) with the task of reaching a settlement with Mexico. Soon after Trist arrived in Mexico, however, Polk lost faith in him and ordered him back to the United States. Trist ignored Polk's orders and continued negotiations with Mexican President Santa Anna. On February 2, 1848, Trist and Mexican officials signed a treaty in the Mexico City suburb of Guadalupe Hidalgo, ending the war.

In retrospect, the treaty seems a major victory for the United States. In return for $18 million ($15 million in outright payment and $3 million to cancel debts Mexico owed to American citizens), Mexico ceded to the United States about half a million square miles of land—an area almost as large as the Louisiana Purchase of 1803. Eventually, all or part of the states of Arizona, California, Colorado, New Mexico, Utah, and Wyoming were created from this "Mexican Cession."

But at the time, few American politicians were satisfied with the treaty. Some Western and Southern congressmen believed the United States, the clear winner on the battlefield, should have demanded all of Mexico. Other Americans, especially in the North, feared that the land won from Mexico would simply provide new territory for slavery. Despite the lukewarm reaction, Polk asked the Senate for ratification. The Treaty of Guadalupe Hidalgo became law on July 4, 1848.

This cartoon (opposite, top) mocks the greed of those Americans who felt that even more land should have been seized from Mexico following the American victory. It shows a smirking Nicholas Trist pointing to all of Mexico and announcing the United States will accept "nothin' shorter."

The area on this map (opposite, bottom) marked "Mexican Cession" is the land gained from Mexico by the Treaty of Guadalupe Hidalgo. As with the Louisiana Purchase, the exact borders of the territory were hard to determine. An American survey team fixed the border between Mexico and the United States in 1851, but disputes over small strips of land continued for decades.

X I C O
GULF OF MEXICO
TEXAS

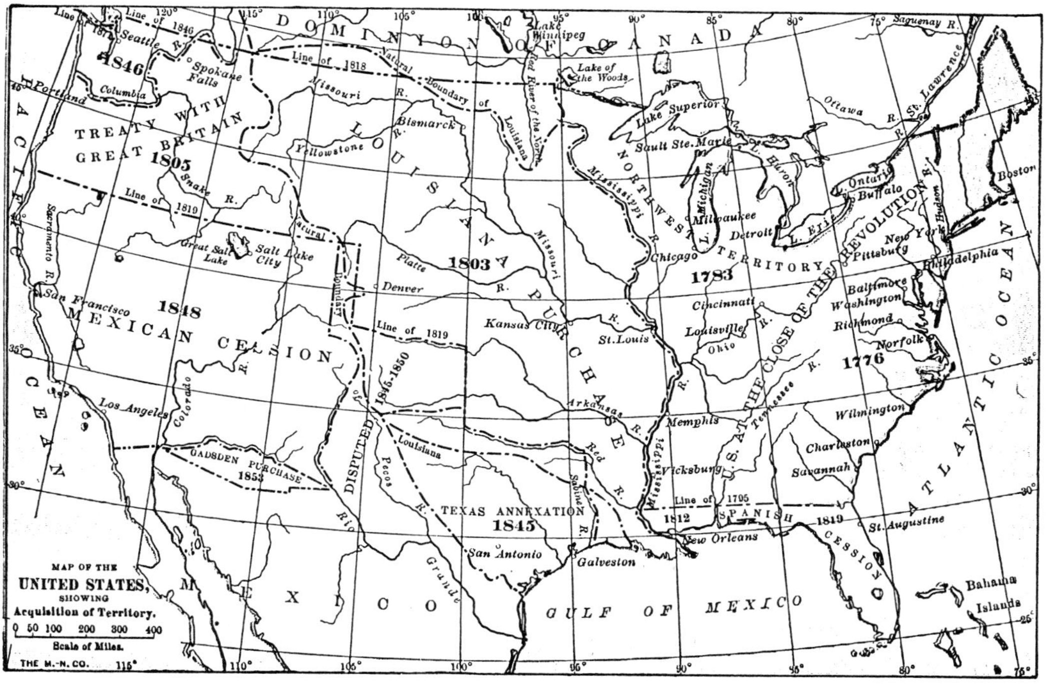
MAP OF THE
UNITED STATES,
SHOWING
Acquisition of Territory.
0 50 100 200 300 400
Scale of Miles.
THE M.-N. CO.
DOMINION OF CANADA
Line of 1846
1846
Seattle
Spokane Falls
Portland
Columbia
Line of 1818
Natural Boundary of Louisiana
Lake Winnipeg
Lake of the Woods
Red River of the North
Missouri R.
Bismarck
Yellowstone
TREATY WITH GREAT BRITAIN
1805
Snake R.
Line of 1819
LOUISIANA PURCHASE
1803
Great Salt Lake
Salt Lake City
Platte
Denver
Kansas City
St. Louis
Sacramento R.
San Francisco
1848
MEXICAN CESSION
Line of 1819
DISPUTED 1836-1850
Colorado R.
Los Angeles
GADSDEN PURCHASE 1853
Louisiana
Pecos R.
Red R.
Sabine R.
Arkansas R.
TEXAS ANNEXATION
1845
San Antonio
Galveston
Rio Grande
M E X I C O
GULF OF MEXICO
Lake Superior
Sault Ste. Marie
L. Michigan
L. Huron
Milwaukee
Chicago
Detroit
NORTHWEST TERRITORY
1783
Mississippi R.
Ontario
Buffalo
L. Erie
Ottawa R.
St. Lawrence
Saguenay R.
Boston
New York
Hudson
Pittsburg
Philadelphia
Baltimore
Washington
Richmond
Norfolk
Cincinnati
Louisville
Ohio R.
Tennessee R.
1776
U. S. AT THE CLOSE OF THE REVOLUTION
Memphis
Vicksburg
Wilmington
Charleston
Savannah
Line of 1795
1812
New Orleans
SPANISH CESSION
1819
St. Augustine
PACIFIC OCEAN
ATLANTIC OCEAN
Bahama Islands

"FIFTY-FOUR FORTY OR FIGHT!"

In 1818, Britain and the United States had agreed to a "joint occupation" of Oregon. This arrangement had worked well while most of the area's white inhabitants were fur traders operating along the coast. But in the 1840s, hundreds of American settlers began moving into the region along the famous Oregon Trail. Now many Americans called for their government to claim all of Oregon for the United States—not just up to the 49th parallel (the U.S.-Canadian border from the Great Lakes to the Rocky Mountains) but up to latitude 54' 40", much farther north.

In 1844, supporters of the "reoccupation" of Oregon held a convention in Cincinnati, Ohio. One of the conventioneers, William Allen, coined the phrase "Fifty-four Forty or Fight!" to sum up the convention's belief that the United States should back up its claim to Oregon, with force if necessary—a move that might mean another war between America and Britain.

The cry was soon taken up by many Americans, including such prominent Democratic politicians as senators Lewis Cass (1782–1866) of Michigan and Stephen Douglas (1813–61) of Illinois, and James K. Polk, victorious Democratic candidate in the presidential election of 1844.

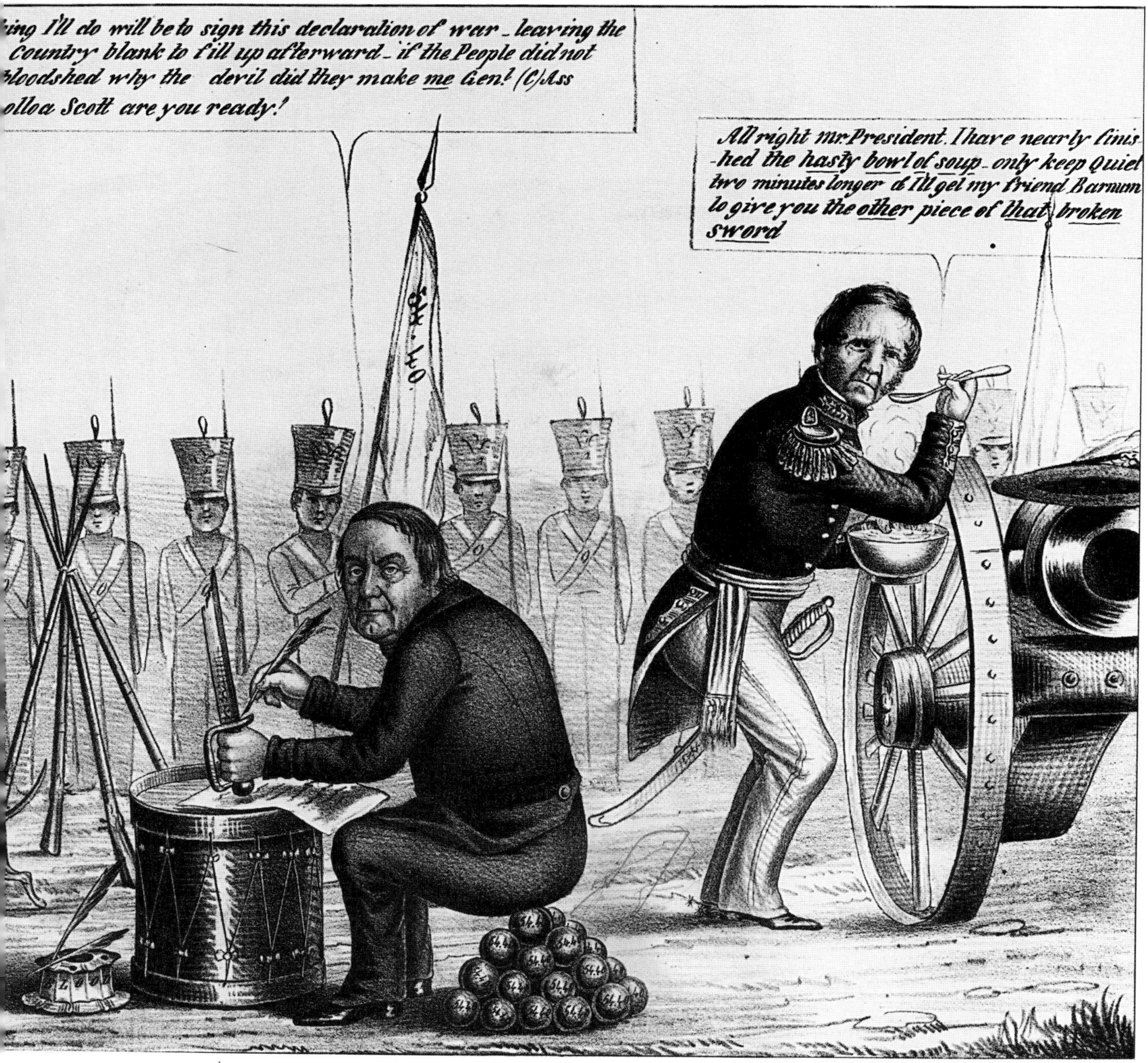

The title of this 1848 cartoon (above)—"President (C)ass Beginning Operations"—pokes fun at the political ambitions of Michigan senator Lewis Cass. Cass made his support for the American claim to Oregon (note the soldier holding a flag marked "54-40") a major theme of his presidential campaign, only to lose to Mexican War hero Zachary Taylor.

SETTLING THE OREGON QUESTION

In 1846, the U.S. government bowed to public pressure and took action on the "Oregon Question." Congress authorized President Polk to inform the British that the "joint occupation" of the region was at an end.

The fact that this action might cause war with Britain meant little to those who wanted Oregon for the United States. In the words of Missouri senator Thomas Hart Benton (1782–1858) "Let the emigrants go on [to Oregon] and carry rifles . . . they will make all quiet there."

But Oregon's value to Britain had fallen when the fur trade ceased to be profitable. The British were therefore willing to compromise. But many people in the United States continued to cry "Fifty-four Forty or Fight!" despite the fact that only a few Americans had settled that far north. President Polk favored the British proposal to divide the territory at the 49th parallel, but he had pledged his support for "all Oregon" in the 1846 election campaign. Eventually, Polk delivered the British proposal to the Senate, which recommended acceptance. Polk was able to save face by "reluctantly" agreeing to the Senate's recommendation. A treaty was signed on June 18, 1846.

The new Oregon Territory included all of what is now Oregon, Washington, Idaho, and a section of Montana, but later these became separate territories. In February 1859, Oregon became the thirty-third state.

The cartoon shown here (above) focuses on the international aspects of the "Oregon Question." Queen Victoria, her husband Prince Albert, and British prime minister the Duke of Wellington warn President Polk (advised by "General Bunkum") to back down on his claim to all Oregon, while a chorus of European leaders add their comments.

THE GADSDEN PURCHASE

By the middle of the nineteenth century, a network of iron rails connected the settled parts of the nation, and railroads soon began to advance into the West. Many Americans believed a transcontinental railroad—one that would connect the West Coast with states east of the Mississippi—was needed.

Congressmen from the South wanted the proposed railroad to be built along a route stretching from their home states to California. This route had the advantage of avoiding the Rocky Mountains, a major obstacle for railroad builders. But there was one problem—the ideal route went through a strip of desert belonging to Mexico.

In 1853, Congress authorized James B. Gadsden (1788–1858), president of the South Carolina Railroad Company, to negotiate with Mexico for this land. Mexican President López de Santa Anna, desperately in need of money, agreed to sell the United States the territory for $10 million. The Gadsden Purchase, as it came to be known, added about 29,000 square miles to the United States. Today, the southern boundary of the purchase marks the border between Mexico and the states of Arizona and New Mexico.

Unfortunately for Gadsden, Southern politicians, and railroad promoters, the Civil War held up construction of the proposed railroad. By the time the railroad (the Southern Pacific) was completed, another transcontinental railroad had been built to the north of the purchase.

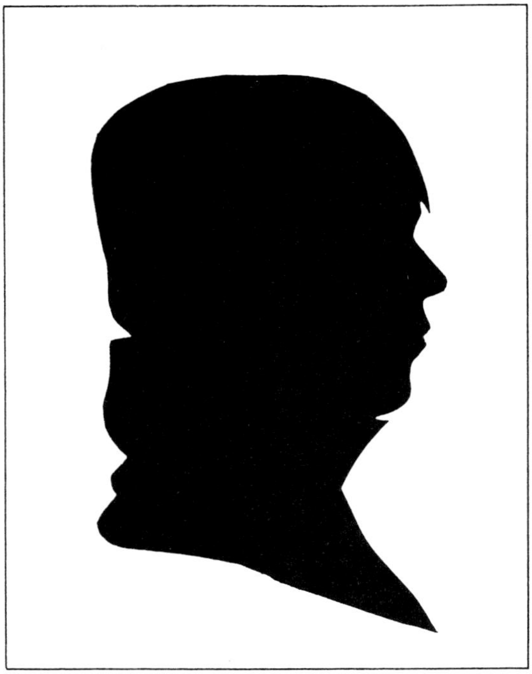

James Gadsden (above in a silhouette portrait) hoped to tie the economy of the new Western states and territories to the South's by building a transcontinental railroad along a southern route. The Civil War and the completion of the Union Pacific–Central Pacific railroad in 1869 frustrated his plans.

Building railroads in the harsh southwestern desert gained by the Gadsden Purchase was a difficult business. This newspaper engraving (right) shows workers, probably employees of the Southern Pacific Railroad, relaxing in their "underground village" along the railroad's single track.

This map shows the land acquired by the Gadsden Purchase of 1853. Although tiny in comparison with the Louisiana Purchase and the Mexican Cession, the Gadsden Purchase is significant—it was the United States's last major gain of land in continental North America.

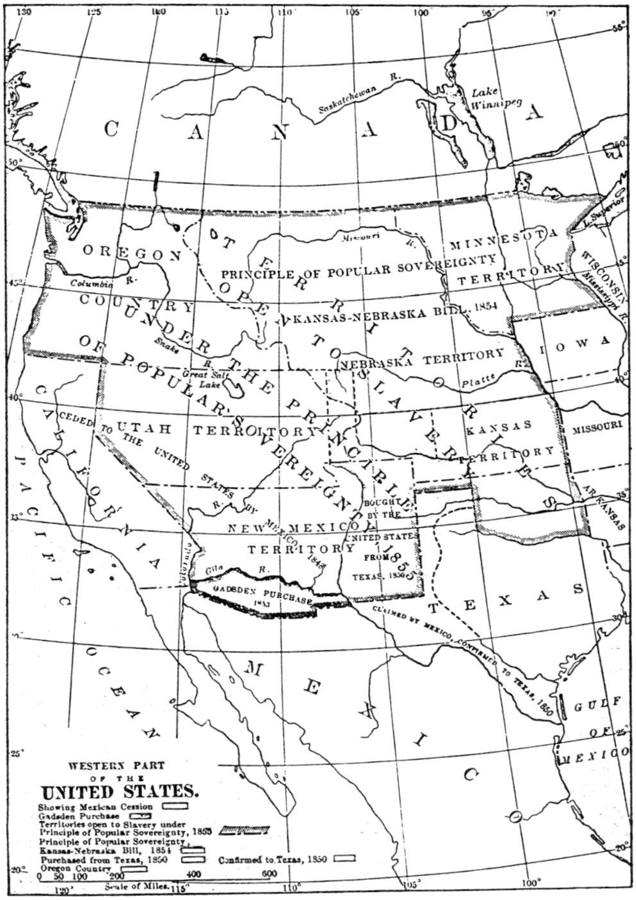

Part III: 1850–1912
The End of the Frontier

By the middle of the nineteenth century, the United States was the supreme power in North America. Lured by gold strikes, religious concerns (like the Mormons who settled Utah), or the simple promise of a new start on free or cheap land, Americans flooded the West. The United States continued to grow.

But a major conflict was brewing. Would slavery be allowed in the West? Missouri's application for statehood in 1817 and California's in 1850, the annexation of Texas in 1846, the victory over Mexico in 1848—each of these events prompted new and increasingly bitter debate over the extension of slavery in the West. In 1861, the nation found itself split in two, and the result was a bloody civil war. The question of slavery in the West was finally answered at Gettysburg and Appomattox.

In 1865, with the Civil War over, the greatest period of Western settlement began. The Homestead Act of 1862 made land readily available; and with railroads providing quick, safe transportation, the steady stream of white settlers grew into a tidal wave. The last major obstacle to settlement was the Native Americans, but soon these proud people retreated, forced into increasingly small "reservations" of land. By 1890, Americans spoke of the "end of the frontier," a phrase popularized in that year by historian Frederick Jackson Turner. Twenty-two years later, the last territories in the continental United States—New Mexico and Arizona—became states. A great, if flawed, chapter of American history—the settlement of the West—was at an end.

Western artist Frederic Remington's painting "The Cavalry Charge" shows U.S. Cavalry troops racing toward their Indian enemies at full gallop. Few actual battles with the Indians resembled this romantized scene.

This map, published in 1910, depicts what early in this century was called the "New West"—the territories that became states during and after the Civil War. These were chiefly the states of the Great Plains and the Southwest. In the early 1800s, many Americans thought these lands would never be permanently settled. Maps of the 1810s and 1820s often labeled the land between the Mississippi River and the Rocky Mountains the Great American Desert. But by the 1870s, the farms and ranches of the Great Plains were feeding the nation, and the mines of the Southwest were pouring out a stream of mineral wealth.

The map shows Arizona and New Mexico as "Territories remaining in 1910." Both were admitted as states in 1912. But these were not the last states to be admitted to the Union.

In 1867, Secretary of State William Seward purchased Alaska from Russia for about $7 million. The treaty finalizing the sale barely passed the Senate; many senators, believing the northern land held few benefits for the nation, called the purchase "Seward's Folly." Alaska formally became a territory in 1912 and a state on January 3, 1959.

The last of the United States was Hawaii. In 1893, the Pacific island kingdom's native monarchy was overthrown. A republic, independent but dominated by American business interests, governed the islands until 1900, when they were annexed to the United States. Hawaii was admitted as the fiftieth state on August 21, 1959.

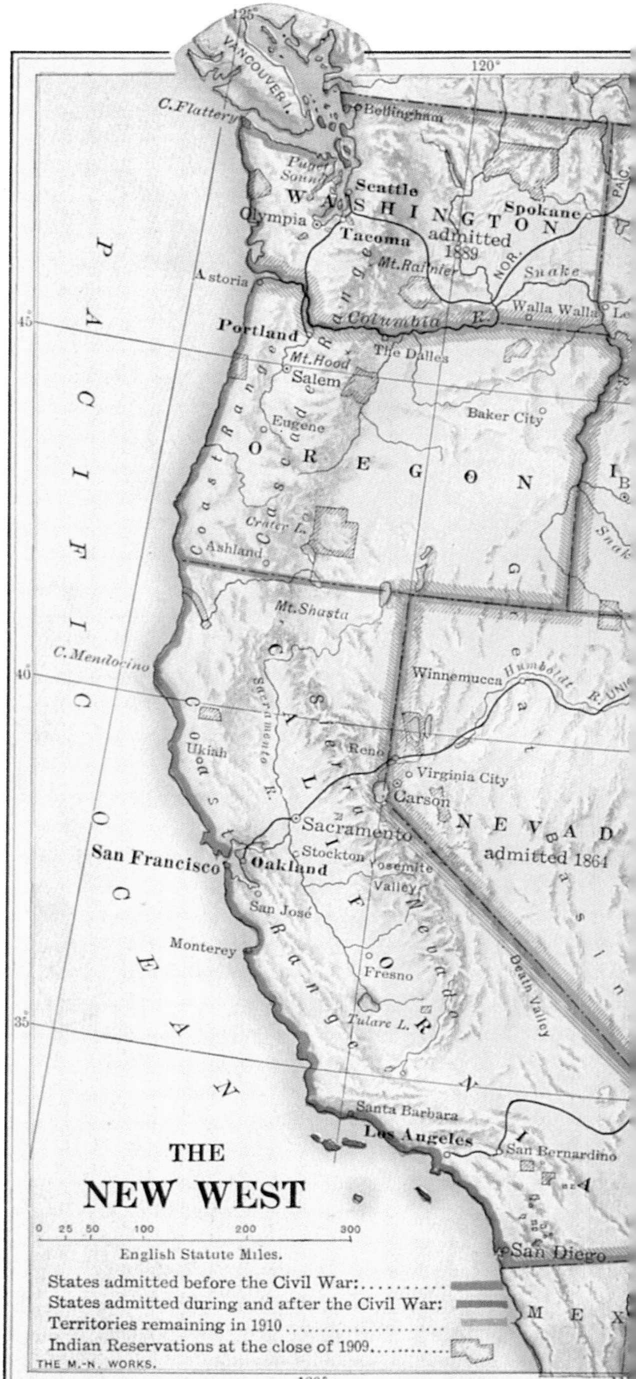

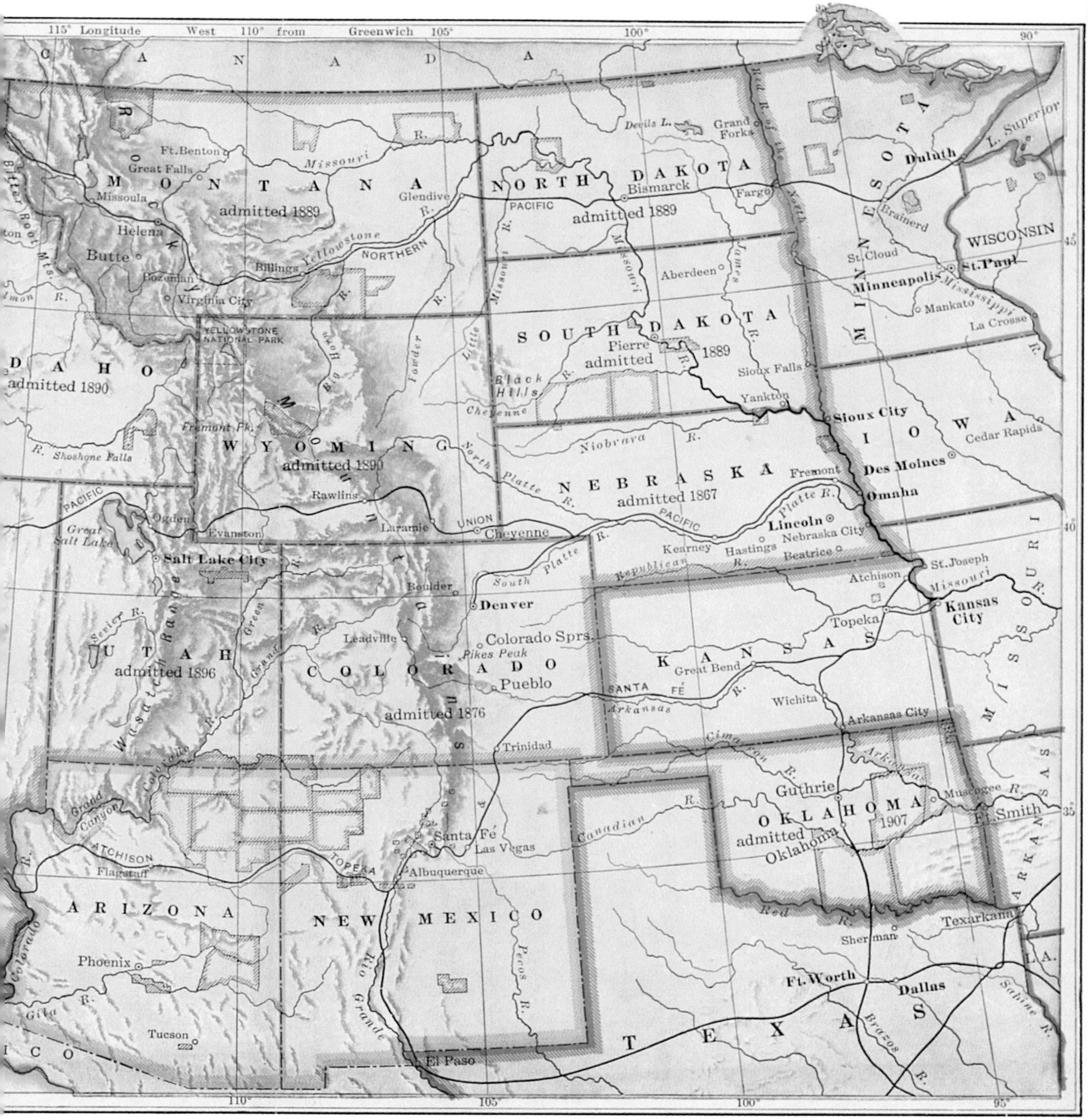
115° Longitude West 110° from Greenwich 105°
100°
90°
C A N A D A
MONTANA
admitted 1889
Ft. Benton
Great Falls
Missoula
Helena
Butte
Bozeman
Virginia City
Billings
Glendive
NORTH DAKOTA
admitted 1889
Bismarck
Devils L.
Grand Forks
Fargo
Duluth
L. Superior
MINNESOTA
Brainerd
St. Cloud
St. Paul
Minneapolis
Mankato
La Crosse
WISCONSIN
SOUTH DAKOTA
admitted 1889
Pierre
Aberdeen
Sioux Falls
Yankton
Black Hills
YELLOWSTONE NATIONAL PARK
IDAHO
admitted 1890
Shoshone Falls
WYOMING
admitted 1890
Fremont Pk.
Rawlins
Ogden
Evanston
Laramie
Cheyenne
Great Salt Lake
Salt Lake City
NEBRASKA
admitted 1867
Fremont
Lincoln
Nebraska City
Kearney
Hastings
Beatrice
Sioux City
IOWA
Cedar Rapids
Des Moines
Omaha
St. Joseph
Atchison
Kansas City
MISSOURI
Topeka
KANSAS
Great Bend
Wichita
Arkansas City
Boulder
Denver
Colorado Sprs.
Pikes Peak
Leadville
Pueblo
COLORADO
admitted 1876
Trinidad
UTAH
admitted 1896
Wasatch Range
Rocky Mts.
Bitter Root Mts.
NORTHERN PACIFIC
UNION PACIFIC
SANTA FÉ
ATCHISON TOPEKA
Missouri
Yellowstone
Big Horn
Powder
Little Missouri
Cheyenne
Niobrara R.
North Platte R.
Platte R.
South Platte
Republican R.
Arkansas
Cimarron R.
Canadian R.
Red R.
Red R. of the North
James R.
Mississippi
Green
Grand
Colorado
Sevier R.
Gila R.
Rio Grande
Pecos R.
Brazos R.
Sabine R.
Guthrie
OKLAHOMA
admitted 1907
Oklahoma
Muscogee
Ft. Smith
ARKANSAS
Texarkana
Sherman
Ft. Worth
Dallas
TEXAS
LA.
Grand Canyon
Santa Fé
Las Vegas
Albuquerque
Flagstaff
ARIZONA
NEW MEXICO
Phoenix
Tucson
El Paso
MEXICO
110°
105°
100°
95°
45°
40°
35°

A TIMELINE OF MAJOR EVENTS

PART III *1850–1912 The End of the Frontier*

UNITED STATES HISTORY

1850 President Taylor dies of cholera and Vice President Millard Fillmore becomes president.
•The District of Columbia abolishes slave trade.
•Congress passes the Fugitive Slave Act. Citizens of free states must now turn in escaped slaves.

1852 *Uncle Tom's Cabin*, by Harriet Beecher Stowe, is published and arouses strong feeling in the nation against slavery.

1854 The newly-formed Republican Party wins more than 100 seats in the House of Representatives, and control of many state governments. Its members oppose the Fugitive Slave Act.

1856 The Republican Party holds its first convention in Philadelphia and nominates John C. Frémont to challenge Democratic candidate James Buchanan.
•Buchanan defeats Frémont in the national presidential election.

1858 Abraham Lincoln runs for the Senate and meets Senator Douglas in a series of seven debates about the slavery issue. Douglas wins the election, but Lincoln gains national attention as an antislavery spokesperson.

1860 Lincoln defeats Stephen Douglas in the presidential election despite his lack of support in the slave states.

1861 Seceding states form a new Southern union called the Confederate States of America, electing Jefferson Davis as their president.
•The U.S. Civil War begins when South Carolina's forces fire on Fort Sumter, South Carolina.

THE CONQUEST OF THE WEST

1850 Congress passes a set of laws called the Compromise of 1850. It admits California as a free state; New Mexico and Utah are organized as territories that will decide themselves whether or not to allow slavery.

1853 Congress authorizes James B. Gadsden to buy 30,000 square miles of land from Mexico. The "Gadsden Purchase" later becomes part of the states of Arizona and New Mexico.

1854 The Kansas-Nebraska Act is passed by Congress. It allows slavery in the territories north of latitude 36' 30" if a majority of settlers vote for it.

1855 Armed conflict between pro- and antislavery settlers breaks out in Kansas.

1857 The U.S. Supreme Court's ruling in the *Dred Scott* case clears the way for slavery in all U.S. territories.

1860 The Pony Express begins carrying mail from St. Joseph, Missouri, to Sacramento, California; it is the nation's first long-distance express mail system.

Pony Express advertisement

1861 Congress forms the territories of Dakota, Nevada, and Colorado.
•The Civil War breaks out. Mississippi, Oregon, California, Kansas, Minnesota, Iowa, and Missouri remain loyal to the Union; Arkansas, Louisiana, and Texas join the Confederacy.

1862 Congress passes the Homestead and Morrill Acts, which provide free Western land to

1862 Over 23,000 troops are killed at the Battle of Antietam, in Maryland, on the bloodiest day of the war.

1865 General Robert E. Lee surrenders to Ulysses S. Grant at Appomattox Courthouse, in Virginia, ending the Civil War.
•President Lincoln is assassinated by John Wilkes Booth, in Washington, D.C. Vice President Andrew Johnson is sworn in as president.
•The 13th Amendment to the Constitution is ratified and slavery is abolished.

1866 The Civil Rights Bill of 1866 is passed to secure equal rights for Southern blacks.

1867 The First Reconstruction Act divides the Southern states into five military districts.

1877 The last federal troops stationed in the South are withdrawn, and the Southern states regain control of their governments.

1896 The Supreme Court rules in *Plessy* v. *Ferguson* that "separate but equal" facilities for blacks and whites are constitutional.

1900 The Foraker Act confirms Puerto Rico as a U.S. territory.

1901 Spanish-American War hero Theodore Roosevelt becomes president of the U.S.

1912 U.S. Marines land in China, Cuba, and Nicaragua to protect U.S. interests.

Booth escaping after the murder of President Lincoln

those willing to settle on it, and federal land to states on which to build colleges, respectively.

1863 The Arizona and Idaho territories are organized.

1864 The Montana Territory is organized; Nevada becomes the thirty-sixth state.

1867 Nebraska becomes the thirty-seventh state.

1868 The Wyoming Territory is organized; a year later, it becomes the first territory to give women the vote.

1877 The Desert Land Act is passed by Congress. The law makes desert land in the Southwest available to settlers who promise to provide irrigation.

1889 Montana and Washington are admitted to the Union as the forty-first and forty-second states.
•The Dakota Territory achieves statehood as two states, North and South Dakota.
•The land between Texas and Kansas, which was supposed to be a permanent Indian territory, begins opening to white settlement.

1890 Idaho and Wyoming become the forty-third and forty-fourth states.
•Congress organizes the Indian Territory as the Oklahoma Territory; nearly 200,000 white settlers arrive between 1889 and 1893.

1896 Utah becomes the forty-fifth state.

1907 Oklahoma is admitted to the Union as the forty-sixth state.

1912 The last territories in the continental United States, New Mexico and Arizona, become the forty-seventh and forty-eighth states.

THE COMPROMISE OF 1850

Debate over whether to allow slavery in land gained from Mexico began even before the Mexican War ended. In 1846, Congressmen David Wilmot (1814–68) of Pennsylvania tried to attach a clause to an otherwise routine law before Congress. If accepted (it wasn't) this "Wilmot Proviso" would have outlawed slavery in all territories ceded by Mexico to the United States.

Wilmot and his supporters were opposed by Southern politicians who wanted the Missouri Compromise, which allowed slavery in territory below latitude 36' 30", to apply to all new Western territories. Debate grew fierce in the late 1840s and finally exploded in January 1850, when the California Territory asked Congress for admission as a free state.

Senator Henry Clay of Kentucky, "the Great Compromiser," offered a solution. Clay's proposals, in the form of five separate bills, finally passed Congress in August and September. Together they became known as the Compromise of 1850. The compromise admitted California as a free state and organized New Mexico and Utah as territories in which the individual populations would vote on whether or not to allow slavery.

The Compromise of 1850 was just that—a compromise. It solved a political crisis, but it didn't end the conflict over slavery in the West—a conflict that grew more bitter every year.

With a sweeping gesture, the eloquent Henry Clay (right, center) argues for the Compromise of 1850 in Congress. The compromise was the last great accomplishment of Clay's political career, which had begun nearly half a century earlier with his election to Congress from Kentucky.

The great Gold Rush of 1848–49 caused California's population to grow so quickly that it was eligible for statehood long before many in Congress expected. In this 1850 lithograph (below), Californians hold a parade in San Francisco, a small town only four years before, to mark the territory's admission as a state.

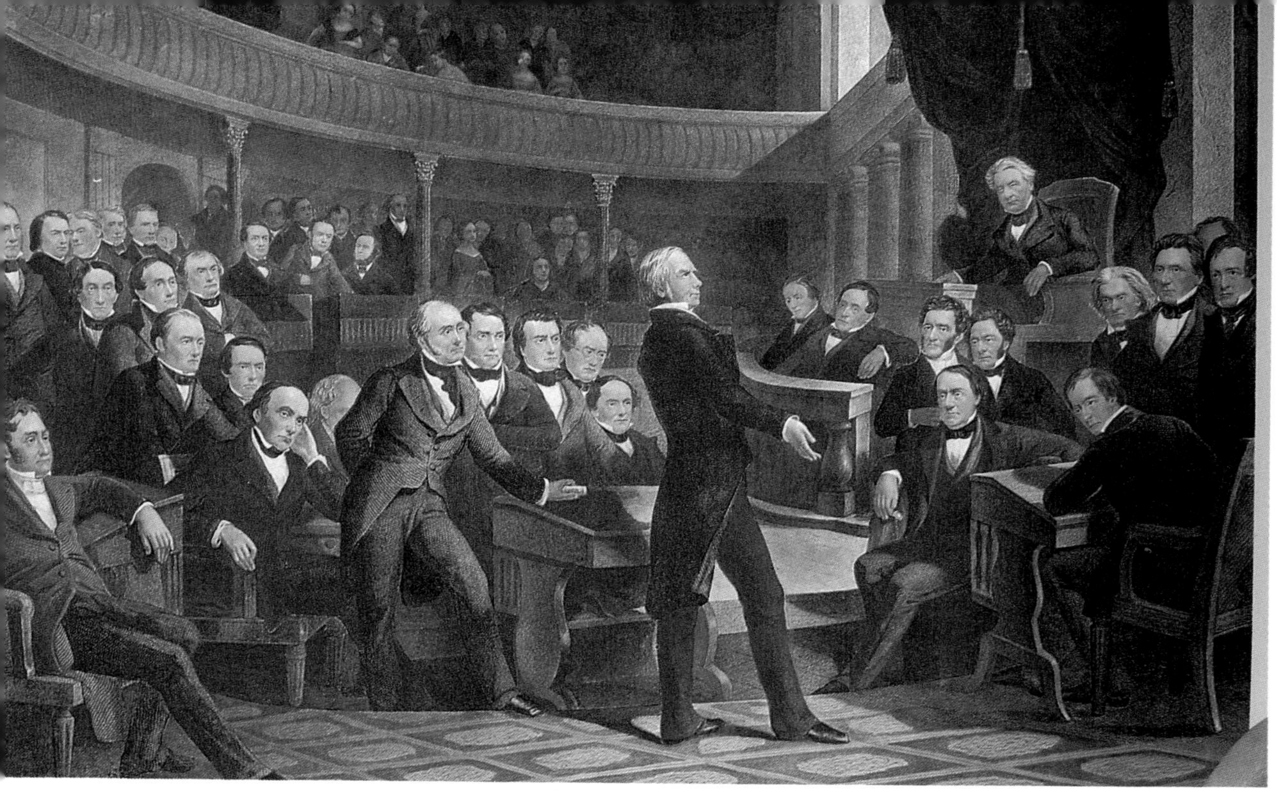

CITY HOTEL

"BLEEDING KANSAS"

In May 1854, Congress passed a bill creating the territories of Kansas and Nebraska out of the land west of Missouri and Iowa. The law called for the citizens of each territory to vote on whether or not to allow slavery—a principle that the bill's sponsor, Senator Stephen Douglas, called "Popular Sovereignty."

Immediately, pro- and antislavery settlers swarmed into the territories. Each side hoped to bring in enough people to win the vote on slavery that would come with elections for a territorial government—but the elections saw fraud on both sides. The first territorial legislature permitted slavery, but antislavery settlers, called "Free Soilers," refused to acknowledge the vote and set up a government of their own.

The battle over slavery was fought with guns as well as with votes. "Border ruffians" from the Southern states clashed with Free Soilers throughout the late 1850s. On May 21, 1856, a proslavery mob practically destroyed the town of Lawrence. But the Free Soilers were also guilty of violence. Four days later, antislavery radical John Brown (1800–59) killed five proslavery settlers at Potawatomie in revenge.

Eventually, it took federal troops and the determination of later territorial governments to bring order to Kansas. The territory became a free state in early 1861. By that time, the entire nation was on the brink of war over the issue of slavery.

"UNION IS STRENGTH."

FREE STATE

CONVENTION!

All who are favorable to union of effort, and a permanent organization of all those who desire to make Kansas a Free State, and who wish to secure, upon the broadest platform, the co-operation of all who agree upon this point, are requested to meet in their respective districts, and appoint Delegates who shall meet in general Convention at

BIG SPRING, THIRD DISTRICT,

On Wednesday, September 5th,

For the purpose of adopting a Platform upon which all may act harmoniously who prefer Freedom to Slavery.

The nomination of a Delegate to Congress, will also come up before the General Convention.

Every District will be entitled to five Delegates for each Representative apportioned by the Governor previously to the last election.

Let no sectional or party issues distract or prevent the perfect co-operation of Free State men. Union and harmony are absolutely necessary to success. The pro-slavery party are fully and effectually organised. No jars nor minor issues divide them. And to contend against them successfully, we also must be united. Without prudence and harmony of action we are certain to fail.

Let every man then do his duty and we are certain of victory.

All Free State men, without distinction, are earnestly requested to take immediate and effective steps to insure a full and correct representation for every District in the Territory.

The Delegates to represent the First and Second Districts in the Convention, will be chosen on the occasion of the

Mass Meeting

To be held at Lawrence on August 14th. The residents of these Districts are requested to attend this meeting.

"United we stand; divided we fall."

By order of the meeting held at Lawrence, July 17, 1855.

["Kansas Free State" Print.]

Antislavery feeling in Kansas was strong in the town of Lawrence. This broadside (above) announces a July 1855 meeting to choose delegates for a convention to be held the following September at the Big Spring settlement. This meeting saw the founding of the "Free-state party," which tried (unsuccessfully) to persuade Congress to admit Kansas as a free state.

One of the last incidents of proslavery versus antislavery fighting in Kansas was also one of the bloodiest. On May 19, 1858, a band of proslavery settlers killed nine "Free Soilers" (opposite, top) near the settlement at Marais de Cygnes.

This violent antislavery cartoon (opposite, bottom) depicts supporters of "popular sovereignty"—including President James Buchanan and Senator Stephen Douglas—as "border ruffians" brutally murdering and scalping "Free Soil" settlers.

RICHARDSON. SC.

Come husband let us go to heaven wh ere our poor Childre en are.
Ho! ho! She thinks I'm her husband, we Scalped the Cus and she like a D..m fool went Crazy on it, and now she wants me to go to heaven with her, ha! ha! ha!
'Twas your's once but its mine now, "Might Makes Right", dont it.
You may bet yer life on that, ole Pud_din head. Come Sis_sy, you go along wid me, I'le take Good care of you (hic), over the left,
O SPARE ME GENTLEMEN, SPARE ME!!
Poor little Dear, We would'nt hurt her for the world, would we Frank? ha! ha! ha! he! he! he! ho! ho! ho!
Hurrah for our side! Victory! Victory! "WE WILL SUBDUE THEM YET"
MARCY
BUCHANAN
PEIRCE
CASS
DOUGLAS
LIBERTY, THE FAIR MAID OF KANSAS_IN THE HANDS OF THE "BORDER RUFFIANS".

SETTLING THE WEST: THE HOMESTEAD ACT

Throughout the nineteenth century, Congress passed laws making public (federally owned) Western land more easily available to those who wanted to settle it. Usually, these "Land Acts" reduced the minimum number of acres that could be sold and lowered the price per acre.

Some Americans wanted Western lands given to settlers for free—especially opponents of slavery, who hoped such a policy would halt the spread of slavery in the West. Southern congressmen, however, defeated attempts to put such a policy into law. After Southern legislators left Congress during the Civil War, President Abraham Lincoln (1809–65) signed the Homestead Act into law. The act, passed in May 1862, gave 160 acres of Western land to "any person who is the head of a family, or who has arrived at the age of twenty-one years, and is a citizen of the United States, or who shall have filed his declaration of intention to become such." To claim their land, settlers had to stay on it for five years and make "improvements."

By the end of the nineteenth century, more than 500,000 settlers had received land under the Homestead Act. While not perfect (Congress had a habit of awarding the best Western land to railroad companies, for example), the Homestead Act probably did more than any other federal law to open the West to permanent, productive settlement.

Among the dangers homesteaders faced was Indian attack, but scenes like the one in this painting (opposite, top), which shows Indian raiders attempting to steal oxen from a wagon train, were fairly rare. White bandits and the harsh nature of the land itself were more of a threat than the Indians, who were increasingly forced onto reservations after the Civil War.

The Homestead Act made it relatively easy to own Western land, but making that land productive was a brutal, backbreaking job. Another danger homesteaders faced was prairie fires. In this engraving (opposite, bottom), a farmer frantically plows a firebreak into his fields in an attempt to prevent a prairie fire from reaching his crops.

POLICING THE WEST

The chief tasks of America's regular army had always been to fight Indians and protect settlers. However, the army's role in the Far West became much more important after the Civil War, when waves of settlers began moving west and conflict with the Indians increased.

The army was small. In 1868, for example, it numbered only 26,000 troops, with the entire West to patrol and protect. The army operated from over 100 forts and posts scattered throughout the Western states and territories. (Contrary to the Hollywood image, the typical Western fort was simply a cluster of barracks and stables rising out of the plains or desert.) It was difficult to find recruits, and usually about a third of the army deserted each year. A private's pay was only thirteen dollars a month in the 1870s, and the frontier army life ranged from extreme boredom during quiet times to extreme danger during campaigns against the Indians, although many soldiers served years without ever seeing combat.

The army fought over 900 engagements against Indians from 1865 to 1890, but fighting the Indians was not its only task. Troops strung telegraph wires, laid rails, helped settlers in times of famine and disaster, and put down riots and other disturbances. In many rowdy Western settlements, the local army post was the only law in the land.

This 1913 painting by Frederic Remington (above), titled "The Stampede" or "Cutting Out a Pony Herd," depicts a common U.S. Cavalry tactic during the wars with the Indians of the Great Plains. While one part of a cavalry unit would attack an Indian village, another detachment stampeded the village's horse herd to make escape impossible.

One of the most dramatic battles of the Indian Wars took place in the Colorado Territory in September 1868, when Cheyenne and Sioux Indians, led by the great chief Roman Nose, trapped about fifty soldiers commanded by Colonel George Forsyth on a small island in the Arickaree River (opposite, top). Forsyth's men fought off repeated attacks until a relief force broke through nine days later.

The officers of the 8th Cavalry Regiment pose for a group portrait at Fort Meade, South Dakota (opposite,bottom). On campaign, the blue uniforms and stiff "forage caps" shown here often gave way to buckskin jackets and wide-brimmed hats.

THE END OF INDIAN TERRITORY

In the 1830s and 1840s, the U.S. government removed 70,000 Indians, mostly members of the "five civilized tribes" (Cherokee, Chickasaw, Choctaw, Creek, and Seminole), from southeastern states and settled them in a vaguely defined region, called the Indian Territory.

By the 1870s, white settlers began illegally moving into this territory. The army tried to keep them out, but the demand that at least part of the Indian Territory be opened to white settlers won out. On April 22, 1889, Congress declared thousands of acres opened to white settlement. Because land was available on a "first come, first served" basis, thousands of people overran the region within days. Their claims, together with some outlying regions, became the Territory of Oklahoma in May 1890.

In 1893, Congress convinced many of the Indian Territory's leading citizens to divide up their remaining tribal lands among individual members—a move that made white settlement in the Indian Territory possible, because Indians could now sell their land.

By 1900, the Oklahoma Territory was ready for statehood. But it made little sense to whites to admit Oklahoma without the Indian Territory, the population of which now included many non-Indians. Some Indians disagreed. At a 1905 conference, the various tribes proposed that the Indian Territory be admitted as state. Congress refused to recognize the proposal. On November 16, 1907, the Oklahoma and Indian territories were admitted as Oklahoma, the forty-sixth state.

GRAND RUSH

FOR THE

INDIAN

TERRITORY!

Over 15,000,000 Acres of Land

NOW OPEN FOR SETTLEMENT!

Being part of the Land bought by the Government in 1866 from the Indians for the Freedmen.

NOW IS THE CHANCE

TO

PROCURE A HOME

In this Beautiful Country!

THE FINEST TIMBER!

THE RICHEST LAND!

THE FINEST WATERED!

WEST OF THE MISSISSIPPI RIVER.

Every person over 21 years of age is entitled to 160 acres, either by pre-emption or homestead, who wishes to settle in the Indian Territory. It is estimated that over Fifty Thousand will move to this Territory in the next ninety days. The Indians are rejoicing to have the whites settle up this country.

The Grand Expedition will Leave Independence May 7, 1879

Independence is situated at the terminus of the Kansas City, Lawrence & Southern Railroad. The citizens of Independence have laid out and made a splendid road to these lands; and they are prepared to furnish emigrants with complete outfits, such as wagons, agricultural implements, dry goods, groceries, lumber and stock. They have also opened an office there for general information to those wishing to go to the Territory. IT COSTS NOTHING TO BECOME A MEMBER OF THIS COLONY.

Persons passing through Kansas City will apply at the office of K. C., L. & S. R. R., opposite Union Depot, for Tickets.

ABOUT THE LANDS.

In answer to inquiries concerning these government lands in the Indian Territory, Col. E. C. Boudinot sends the following from Washington:

FIRST—In reply I will say that the United States, by treaties made in 1866, purchased from Indian tribes, in the Indian Territory, about 14,000,000 acres of land.

SECOND—These lands were bought from the Creeks, Seminoles, Choctaws and Chickasaws, by their treaty of 1866.

The Creeks, by their treaty of 1866, sold to the United States 3,250,560 acres, for the sum of $975,168. The Seminoles, by their treaty of 1866, sold to the United States 2,169,080 acres, for the sum of $325,362.

The Choctaws and Chickasaws, by their treaty of 1866, sold to the United States the "leased lands" lying west of 98 degrees of west longitude, for the sum of $300,000. The number of acres in this tract is not specified in the treaty, but it contains about 7,000,000 acres. (See 14th vol. Statutes at Large, pages 756, 769 and 786.)

Of these ceded lands the United States has since appropriated for the use of the Sac and Foxes 479,667 acres and for the Pottawatomies 575,877 acres, making a total of 1,055,542 acres. These Indians occupy these lands by virtue of treaties and acts of Congress. By an unratified agreement, the Wichita Indians are now occupying 713,610 acres of these ceded lands. I presume some action will be taken by the United States government to permanently locate the Wichitas upon the land they now occupy. The title, however, to these lands is still in the United States.

By executive order, Kiowa, Comanche, Arrapahoe, and other wild Indians, have been brought upon a portion of the ceded lands, but such lands are a part of the public domain of the United States, and have all been surveyed and sectionised.

A portion of these 14,000,000 acres of land, however, has not been appropriated by the United States for the use of other Indians and all probability never will be.

THIRD.—These unappropriated lands are situated immediately west of the 97th degree of west longitude and south of the Cherokee territory. The soil is well adapted for the production of corn, wheat and other cereals. Is is unsurpassed for grazing, and is well watered and timbered.

FOURTH.—The United States have an absolute and unembarrassed title to every acre of these 14,000,000 acres, unless it be to the 1,054,544 now occupied by the Sac and Fox and Pottawatomie Indians. The Indian title has been extinguished. The articles of the treaties with the Creeks and Seminoles, by which they sold their lands, begin with the statement that the lands are ceded "in compliance with the desire of the United States to locate other Indians and freedmen thereon." By the express terms of these treaties the lands bought by the United States were not intended for the exclusive use of other Indians" as has been so often asserted. They were bought as much for the negroes of the country as for Indians.

DISTANCES FROM INDEPENDENCE,

Via Old Government Road, to Government Land in the Indian Territory:

Independence, Kansas	Good Wood and Water	CAMP GROUND
Onion Creek	5 Miles	Wood and water.
Hickory Creek	10 Miles	Wood and water.
California Creek	18 Miles	Wood and water.
Brush Creek	28 Miles	Wood and water.
Big Cana River	38 Miles	Wood and water.
Double Creek	43 Miles	Wood and water.
Bird Creek	53 Miles	Wood and water.
Hominy Creek	60 Miles	Wood and water.
Delaware Creek	63 Miles	Wood and water.
Arkansas Riv. (Bruner's Crossing)	70 Miles	Wood and water.
Rock Creek	82 Miles	Wood and water.
Double Pole Cat Creek	94 Miles	Wood and water.
Post Oak Creek	109 Miles	Wood and water.
Deep Fork Creek	131 Miles	Wood and water.
Sac and Fox Agency	134 Miles	West side Deep Fork Creek.
Cimaron River	150 Miles	North line Government Lands.

ADDRESS

WM. C. BRANHAM,

Independence, Kansas.

To parties accompanying my Colony, I would advise them to purchase their Outfit at Independence, Kas., I have examined Stock and Prices of Goods, such as Wagons, Plows, Lumber, Dry Goods, Groceries, and, in fact, everything that is needed by Parties settling upon new Land, and find them as cheap as they can be bought in the East.

RESPECTFULLY YOURS,

Col. C. C. CARPENTER.

P. S.—Parties will have no trouble in getting transportation at Independence for hauling their goods into the Territory. C. C. C.

Posters—like this one (left), published in Kansas in 1879—were circulated throughout the West as land in the Indian Territory became available for settlement. While much of the land in the Indian Territory was fertile, the glowing description in the poster was a typical exaggeration by speculators hoping to get rich selling lots to gullible newcomers.

One of the most coveted lands in the Indian Territory was the Cherokee Strip, 12,000 square miles set aside for that tribe's use in 1833. In 1893, the federal government purchased it for $8.5 million and opened it to white settlement. At noon on September 16 of that year, settlers raced into the area (below) to stake their claims.

THE LAST TERRITORIES BECOME STATES

By 1908, only two territories remained in the West—Arizona and New Mexico, both regions that had been acquired from Mexico. Most of the land that made up these territories was ceded to the United States in the Treaty of Guadalupe Hidalgo; the Gadsden Purchase of 1853 provided the rest.

Both New Mexico and Arizona had achieved territorial status in 1863. American settlement in New Mexico had begun even before the Mexican War, thanks to the Santa Fe Trail, one of the major trade routes of the West. After the Civil War, New Mexico's grasslands provided the base for many great cattle ranches.

Settlement in Arizona was slower. With rugged mountains to the north and a blazing desert in the south, Arizona was inhospitable. "Everything here either bites or stings," wrote an army officer stationed in the territory. But by 1886, more settlers were arriving in Arizona, many lured by the territory's mineral wealth.

A proposal to admit both territories as a single state was defeated, and Arizona and New Mexico entered the Union separately in 1912. New Mexico became the forty-seventh state on January 6; Arizona followed as the forty-eighth on February 14.

Pioneering photographer Alexander Gardner took this photograph (below) of Arizona's Canyon de Chelly while accompanying a government surveying expedition. The canyon, typical of the harsh but beautiful landscape found in Arizona and New Mexico, is today part of the Navajo Indian reservation.

Resource Guide

Key to picture positions: (T) top, (C) center, (B) bottom; and in combinations: (TL) top left, (TC) top center, (TR) top right, (BL) bottom left, (BC) bottom center, (BR) bottom right, (CR) center right, (CL) center left.

Key to picture locations within the Library of Congress collections (and where available, photo negative numbers): P - Prints and Photographs; HABS - Historical American Buildings Survey (div. of Prints and Photographs); R - Rare Book Division; G - General Collections; MSS - Manuscript Division; G&M - Geography and Map Division.

PICTURES IN THIS VOLUME

2-3 San Francisco, P **4-5** Medal, G **6-7** Jefferson, P

Part I: **8-9** Boone, **10-11** C, map, G **12-13** TL, road, G; BL, Jefferson, P; TR, Jackson, P, USZ62-205; BR, map, G **14-15** TL, census, P; BL, map, G; TR, debate, P; BR, Alamo, P, USZ62-13598 **16-17** TL, Wayne, P, USZ62-56544; TR, Ft. McIntosh, R; BR, map, G&M **18-19** TL, document, MSS; TR, map, G&M; BR, reading, P, USZ62-17891 **20-21** TL, Wilkinson, P; TR, McCullogh, P; BR, Pioneers, P, USZ62-53341 **22-23** TL, Serra, R; TR, mission, P, USZ62-7918; BR, Presidio, P, USZ62-03253 **24-25** T, outpost, P, USZ62-7919; B, logbook, P, USZ62-7279 **26-27** TL, Morales, P; BR, New Orleans, P, USZ62-1660 **28-29** TL, Livingston, P; TR, Louisiana Purchase, P, USZ62-16078 **30-31** TR, document, P; BR, Lewis and Clark, P, USZ62-17372 **32-33** TL, Clay, P; TR, Benton, P, USZ62-1112; BR, camp plan, P **34-35** TL, Tecumseh, P, USZ62-8255; TR, Dearborn, P, USZ62-73797; BR, Ft. Detroit, P, USZ62-9290 **36-37** TL, song, MSS; TR, Jackson, P; BR, battle, P, USZ62-25963 **38-39** C, riot, P, USZ62-10294 **40-41** TL, letter, MSS; TR, San Antonio, R; BC, Stephen, P, USZ62-206; BR, Moses, P

Part II: **42-43** Scott, P **44-45** TL, poster, P, USZ62-5550; BL, Palo Alto, P; TR, notice, G; BR, Monterey, P **46-47** TL, Greeley, P; TR, cartoon, P, USZ62-9917; BR, Mormons, P, USZ62-39803 **48-49** TL, Bowie, P; TR, Crockett, P; BC, Alamo, P, USZ62-222 **50-51** C, cartoon, P, USZ62-1273 **52-53** TR, cartoon, P, USZ62-10802; BR, cockfighting, P **54-55** TL, Polk, P; BL, Slidell, P, B184-10310; BR, porch, P, USZ62-90415MB **56-57** C, Palo Alto, P **58-59** BL, Monterey, P; TR, Buena Vista, P **60-61** TR, Frémont, P, USZ62-049597; BC, San Diego, G **62-63** BC, Sacramento, P; TR, Kearny, P, USZ62-17905 64-65 TL,Cerro Gordo, P, USZ62-13650; TR, bombardment, P; BR, Veracruz, P **66-67** TR, Chapultepec, P, USZC4-622; BR, Scott, P **68-69** TR, cartoon, P; BR, map, G 70-71 TC, cartoon, P, USZ62-062678 **72-73** TC, Oregon cartoon, P, USZ62-7722 **74-75** TL, Gadsden, G; TR, map, G; BR, railroad, P, USZ62-721

Part III: **76-77** Cavalry, P **78-79** C, map, G **80-81** BL, advertisement, G; TR, Booth, P, USZ62-8675 **82-83** TR, Clay, P, USZ62-689; BC, parade, P, USZ62-763 **84-85** TL, document, P, USZ62-2806; TR, massacre, P, USZ62-33382Q; BR, cartoon, P, USZ62-52003 **86-87** TR, wagons, P; BR, fire, P **88-89** TL, cavalry, P; TR, battle, P; BR, officers, P, USZ62-058836 **90-91** TL, poster, P, USZ62-11487; BC, land rush, P, USZ62-801 **92-93** C, canyon, P

SUGGESTED READING

The American Heritage Illustrated History of the United States, volumes 6 and 7. New York: American Heritage, 1988.

American Heritage. *Westward to the Oregon Trail.* Mahwah, N.J.: Troll Associates, 1987.

Daniel, Clifton. *Chronicle of America.* New York: Prentice Hall, 1989.

Josephy, Alvin M. Jr. *The World Almanac of the American West.* New York: Pharos Books, 1986.

Miller, Marilyn. *The Transcontinental Railroad.* New York: Silver Burdett, 1986.

Morrison, Samuel. *The Oxford History of the American People.* New York: Oxford University Press, 1965.

Ochoa, George. *The Fall of Mexico City.* New York: Silver Burdett, 1989.

Wills, Charles. *The Battle of Little Bighorn.* New York: Silver Burdett, 1990.

Index

Page numbers in *italics* indicate illustrations